# The Last, Best Lessons:
# A Way of Aging

Roberta Culbertson, Ph.D.

*Based on the Discoveries of Sarah Z.*

Roberta A. Culbertson© 2021
Manufactured in the United States of America
All rights reserved.

Cover and Interior Design: Angela "Silver Star" Daniel
Cover Photo: Erica Rothman
Printer and Binder: Lulu

Culbertson, Roberta A.

*The Last, Best Lessons: A Way of Aging*
978-1-365-21211-6

R O A D

RESPONSIBLE OLD AGE AND DEATH

ROAD Press
Responsible Old Age and Death, LLC
*www.responsibleoldageanddeath.com*

# To Sarah Z.
*Collaborator, Friend, Inspiration*

# Foreword:
# The Last, Best Lessons:
# A Way of Aging

What challenges face us as we age? What does it look like to be in control of your life? The decisions you make each day about how you prefer to live and work and play? To what extent are you in charge of your life's daily activities...and... what would it be like to lose that daily control to aging or illness and infirmity? How could that loss be dealt with in a way that maintains personal dignity and choice?

These are the underlying themes that introduce the reader to Sarah Z., a powerful, accomplished, management consultant who entered her final twenty plus years of life as a woman afflicted with a degenerative neurological disease and who, little by little, lost her sense of personal physical agency and with it, the loss of the vibrant and productive life of her first fifty years.

Being acutely aware of how her Parkinson's disease, diagnosed at age 51, was progressing with age, Sarah Z. took every step she could to mitigate its effects and to live life to the fullest. She even underwent Deep Brain Stimulation surgery, embedding a neurotransmitter in her chest that was wired to the part of her brain controlling movement, allowing her to suffer fewer consequences of massive doses of synthetic dopamine as she entered her mid-60s. It was miraculous how her dyskinesia seemed to vanish after that procedure. This story details her journey to a continuing care retirement community, also called a lifespan community, when, after aging with Parkinson's disease was taking a greater and greater toll on her autonomy, the lure of a facility in which to age became very appealing.

What happened as Sarah's physical abilities continued to decline is at the heart of this story of aging into death. What if we could take control of our process of dying as we did of our process of living? Why do these senior communities have to be run in ways that deny the individual histories and stories of those whose bodies are failing them? Why do the elderly appear to be lumped together into one amorphous whole in the best of these facilities and how might it look different? And...finally, why can't there be more choices for a peaceful death?

As Sarah's story unfolds, it becomes clear that the loss of autonomy and the inability to engage in the experiences that make life meaningful became her driving force to imagine a better way of advancing into old age and saying goodbye with dignity. This is not a book about dying. It is a book about living one's best life and taking control of its inevitable end.

*Janice Koch, Ph.D.*
*Professor Emerita*
*Hofstra University*
*Long Island, New York*

# Acknowledgments

First, I deeply appreciate the collaboration, support, editing and ideas of my colleague, Catherine Wetherby. Catherine and I worked with Sara Z. for more than a year, and then worked on the book together for over two years. Catherine read every word several times and helped to articulate or expand many key concepts. She kept up with the burgeoning current literature and compiled the resources section at the end of the book. As a collaborator and friend, she is the best.

Sarah's friend Janice Koch, who wrote the foreword, was with us all the way through Sarah's death and became a main editor and guide for the book itself. She was unfailing in her support, frank in her corrections and clarifications, and a true collaborator in building the structure and voice of the text. But Janice was more than a source of information about Parkinson's, Sarah's personality and her life; she became a lifelong friend. As she said, Sarah gave us to one another.

Angela "Silver Star" Daniel, with whom I have worked for over two decades, took the text and turned it into a work of art. Her patience and quiet competence again made the cover design and layout both professional and beautiful. She also handled all publishing issues, making the whole process appear seamless.

Joyce Allan and Laura Shears—coming from different experiences of aging themselves—read the text and offered frank and detailed suggestions and comments. I am grateful they didn't hold back on critique and that they offered support in many other ways.

Latifa Kropf knew Sarah at the end of her life, at the time of her spiritual discoveries. Latifa shared her experiences and insights about this most important process of Sarah's movement toward death, enlivening the book and keeping the writing honest.

Joyce Allan helped us to understand end-of-life matters and the complexities of the decisions that must be made.

Erica Rothman's photograph belonged to Sarah, who gave it to Catherine. Ms. Rothman graciously allowed us to use it for the cover. It captures not only Sarah's love of art and detail, but also helps to bring alive the concept of Sarah's Window.

Miles Lee drew the beautiful image of Sarah's Window, based on the window in Erica Rothman's photograph.

I am grateful for the support of my family, who offered me a quiet place to work and listened to the whining and confused ideas that have punctuated family gatherings for two years. My sister-in-law guided me to the title after much struggle on my part. They have also asked me the hard questions I hope this book will evoke in all of us. My daughters took on the changes I made in my own approach to death with their usual incisiveness and care; we have had many conversations about how I want to treat them as I age.

My friends Will Sinclair and Ruth Hodges reminded me

to take time to refresh and relax; all my friends at Farm Colony gave me the freedom from community chores to work as I needed to finish this book. I am grateful for a community and way of life that allow such freedom amid such support. In particular, I thank Deborah Lee for her unfailing support of whatever I do, and our many conversations that found their way into these pages.

Finally, to my dog Roan—constant companion, quiet, unassuming, and wise beyond my years—and to my chickens, who remind me that humans are pretty much just big chickens with slightly better manners.

# Table of Contents

# Sacred Heart, Listening Heart

*I have been sad about aging. Not because I have some idealized version of youth. Actually it's hard to put into words what I have thought I was losing. It seems to be a gallant fight that each of us has to lose....*

*So, I asked God for the umpteenth time: What can I do with the rest of my life that will have real meaning? That will help younger people to see old age as something to look forward to, something to learn, to earn, to achieve, to contribute from?*

*Finally, an answer came that I think will get me out of bed in the morning. A true sacred vision: to develop a listening heart.*

*The older I get, the better I can be a listening heart both for myself and for others. A listening heart is the amniotic fluid, the ideal food source for a person who has already been born to continue to grow. Perhaps I can stop seeing myself as someone who in the unavoidable process of aging is also becoming less. Perhaps, instead of monitoring all the things I can no long DO in the world, I can expand and develop what I can BE in the world— for myself, my children, my grandchildren, and others who may benefit from the presence of a listening heart. Fortunately, I don't think that is something I will age out of.*

*Sarah Z.*

1

# Introduction

*If we are lives and souls to keep*
*If we are Love, I hope we do not sleep*
*I hope we do not sleep, I hope we stay our ground*
*Hold fast to the mother as she turns us 'round*

*– Ferron, lyrics from "The Cart"*

This book begins with one woman's journey through aging and into her death—for which she was prepared and not prepared. She had had Parkinson's for over twenty years but remained vital, even if physically failing, to her last day. She had long ago determined to depart her life when it became clear that thenceforth she could live only as someone she would not recognize and whom others would be pained to see. She had thought she was ready.

But the last parts of her life proved more chaotic, more nuanced, more rife with unexpected everyday crises and completely unexpected struggles than she had expected. Nor had she anticipated the day-to-day grind of aging— the constant downhill, almost violent but seemingly never-ending ride.

Sarah hadn't expected to find just how much she had to surrender in exchange for care; how the aging can be treated unfairly; and how the lessons of old age are easy to miss or ignore because one doesn't recognize them. She struggled with fears and anger of all dimensions.

Even so, it was not all desperate discoveries of what she left undone or insufficiently understood; some unexpected good emerged with the bad. Near the end of her life, Sarah found a peace and happiness that often had eluded her in her lifetime. Her last days were not rosy or mystical; it wasn't as if she basked in endless sunshine toward the end. The road to heaven did not open, nor every grief subside. Her peace and happiness were quiet and simple, even fun and clear. They made her courageous in the face of pain and death. The manner of her last months and death reflected the person she had always wanted to be: no more, and no less.

As Sarah made her many discoveries, she decided she wanted others to know what they might face, and so this book was born.

The remainder of this book offers ways to use Sarah's discoveries for ourselves. They are a window into the aging process that almost everyone will someday face. Sarah's experiences look outward to what is coming, and inward to what each of us might bring to it. "Sarah's Window" provides tools to help others generate the personal vision and discipline to prepare for their own aging and dying.

With attention, it is possible to anticipate and mentally, emotionally, and deeply prepare for the shocks, unwelcome changes, and even deep grief that will come as adulthood becomes something entirely different called "old age." It is important to think carefully about financial and family preparation. But most important, studying what is to come can help to take advantage of our last chance to learn about life. For whatever it will bring in terms of difficulty, and sometimes because of it, aging into death can also offer a deeper maturation and a rediscovery of who we really are.

Sarah wanted to point out that while we might see what she had learned and the lessons that followed as if they were a distant truck far behind us in the sideview mirror, the objects were closer than they appeared.

With the tools here, you can begin to be realistic—and optimistic—about what is to come. But first, Sarah's story.

**How the Book Will Unfold**

The first three chapters introduce the topics of aging and dying—and Sarah Z. herself.

Beginning with Chapter Four, we will delve into Sarah Z.'s four major discoveries, how she made them, and what lessons she learned from them. Each discovery has many facets, and each was a struggle. In her first discovery, described in Chapter Four, "Freedom and Surrender," Sarah was deeply shocked that much, and finally everything she had and was, must be given up as we age and then die. As she lost her physical and mental abilities, she lost her freedom, and surrendered much she valued in order to be "cared for." The second of Sarah's discoveries, described in Chapter Five, "Respect and Relevance," was that her desires to contribute were hindered by discrimination against the aging. She fought a culture and institutions that labeled old people as weak and often useless.

In Chapter Six, "Going Deep—Questions and Answers," Sarah's discoveries added a parallel, lighter track to her darkness and anger. She discovered that she could ask questions of herself about what was truly important, and that surrender came in many forms. Chapter Seven, "The Last, Best Lessons—Caring and Connecting," shows that rather than Sarah's discovery of something grand at the end of her life, she found something much quieter and personal: a more open sense of life and a kind of love she had longed for her whole life. Chapter Eight, "Leaving," takes Sarah through the leadup to her death, the many decisions she discovered she must make, and how she made them

Chapters Nine and Ten, "Sarah's Window—A Practical Way of Aging," and "A Spiritual Way of Aging," bring Sarah's discoveries into our own lives in a way we can use them to plan, prepare for, and learn from the final stage of life.

# Chapter One:
# A Surprising Expected Death

*When your time comes to die, be not like those whose hearts are filled with fear of death...Sing your death song and die like a hero going home.*

*Tecumseh, Shawnee Warrior and Chief*

**August 9**

A rainy Friday evening. After a long day of work as a chaplain at a retirement facility, I had little left for myself. I wanted a steak and a glass of wine and some deadening TV, and nothing to do with sad things. I was standing in the checkout line at the grocery store, consulting the Betty and Veronica comic books and exulting in the promise of a whole weekend of downtime before me when my phone rang. I hate when people talk on the phone in the grocery line, but I saw who it was and knew I had to take it. "Sarah's in the hospital," my friend said. "She's declined treatment and her kids are on board with it. They have her advance directive with them. She's disconnected her neurotransmitter too, so she's pretty much looking at the end now. Hospice is here." I was at the cashier; I said I'd call her back, just as the baking potato and the big ribeye rode by on the belt. I couldn't think. I checked out on automatic pilot.

Outside in the car I called my friend back. A nurse by training, she offered up more details: "Sarah's gotten a virus, they think; she can't hold her medicine down, so her Parkinson's is getting worse. They could hydrate her, which would help, but she's said no. She says it's time." I asked the logical question and my friend responded; "They can't say exactly, of course, maybe a day or two, maybe a couple more. Not much past that." A long time for Sarah. Much as my tired body fought me, I dutifully asked if I should go to the hospital now. "No," my friend said, "I'm here—you come in the morning. Her kids are here and they're holding up okay." I was shamefully relieved about that part—I told myself I would have gone had she said yes.

A grocery store parking lot at dusk in a driving rain is a dolorous place; I sat there as the windows fogged and worried rather too much about whether or not it still would be fun to eat the steak.

Then, there it was again, like a bell tolling: "Sarah's dying!" The fact began to leap into my stomach every few minutes, followed by numbness again and ridiculous concerns like where I might park tomorrow at the hospital. I drove home fading in and out hypnotically, except when the potholes sprayed water up to the windows with a roar. Sarah! I stared at the road through the wipers, now on high, and tried to take the curves with more care than usual as I knew I wasn't quite myself.

How could this have happened? We knew it was going to, but...is anybody ever really ready? What would we do without her dear, funny, honest, strong self in the world? And she, how was she at this moment? What hurt? What could she see? Was she dreaming? Could she see her children? Was she happy? She knew she was dying: the answers to all those questions she had asked about life and death—were they all coming to her now?

Finally, I reached home, turned the engine off, and sat there in the stillness, except for the rain hammering on the roof. I couldn't get out yet. Sitting in the car I called my colleague and friend, Catherine. We had been working with Sarah together, and Sarah had tasked us with producing the book she wanted to leave behind. There was a lot to consider in the moment. I gave Catherine the details.

We soon ran out of things to say and felt a growing quiet. What else could we do? Catherine sighed after a while. "We'll hold her in the Light, as the Quakers say."

Parkinson's medicine, treatments and therapeutics are nearly miraculous until they aren't anymore. Then the end is terrible; in part, an effect of the withdrawal of the medications that no longer work. Sarah wanted to die as herself, not as a disease. She had been wanting, and finally had laid plans to leave the Earth when she felt herself slipping into the last chaotic stages of her disease. She wanted to do this as a matter of her own personal pride and sense of herself, but also to spare her family and the others who loved her the pain of witnessing the powerlessness and grief of that ignominious end.

Sarah's plan had been this: In a month's time, in

September, after she had said her goodbyes and made peace where she needed, she would put an end to her treatments. She would stop her Parkinson's medications, and turn off the mechanism that controlled the neurotransmitter placed in her brain during Deep Brain Stimulation surgery (DBS) a few years before. These two therapies had been keeping her from experiencing the full-blown last-stage effects of Parkinson's Disease. She would not be able to eat and drink once she ceased these. She would die after that, though it was hard to say exactly when; overall the estimate was some three to five days, or perhaps a bit longer. She had a right to stop her treatments; she did not legally have a right to any help to end her life. So, she would go it alone until hospice could step in—which would be when she was clearly about to die. Parkinson's is cruel in this way; it doesn't "kill" a person until it has destroyed the body's ability to think, move, talk, eat, and otherwise be human. Most often, something like pneumonia, a stroke, or a virus snuffs out the last glimmer somewhere in that process, but it was hard to know just when that might happen. Sarah was expecting the end to be difficult, lonely, and terrible, but she was ready. It was time, after a long time, to say goodbye to a life that was soon to be barely hers anymore.

And so, we had expected her to make her move soon, but not yet. She was supposed to make that move, not some nameless piece of RNA that had invaded her body by chance and taken it over.

We should have known that humans do not often have

the final word in such matters. It is said, "Man proposes; God disposes." Death, it seemed, had its own plans: Sarah's end would be partly hers to arrange, but Death would decide the date. Now it had, and she was going very soon.

We hoped there would be time for us to say goodbye. We resolved to go to the hospital together early in the morning and offer whatever we could in the way of help or farewells.

### August 10

Saturday: Catherine and I met around 8:00 in the morning and headed into town. In the night, she had been transferred to her nursing facility. Hospice was managing her care. We stepped out of the elevator into the relative quiet of the floor, the carpet absorbing sounds, and the rooms, with other people close to death or ill, also quiet.

We were not the first to stand outside Sarah's door that morning. There was nearly a line, each of us waiting patiently to be invited in. After a short time, we were.

The room was dark but comfortable. Sarah was on a bed lowered to the floor; a fall would not hurt her from that height of a few inches. But falling out of her bed three feet off the floor in her room—*that* had been a common and dangerous occurrence as her illness had progressed. Suddenly I had a flash of anger; why had her bed not been on the floor all that time? It could have been raised and lowered as she needed! Of course, the matter was irrelevant now, but I was angry. As minds can do in unusual and distressing circumstances, mine was trying desperately to change the subject. For its own stability it wanted to distract me from the situation that Catherine and I were now an intimate part of. Who knew what I might do at that moment? Cry? No. In my family, we don't cry.

Sarah's daughters sat nearby and watched their mother like bear cubs. They called immediately for whatever she seemed to need: more medication for pain or control of her body, another pillow, ice chips.

It is always somewhat startling to see a true "deathbed." This would be Sarah's last time to speak, love, sleep, dream...and breathe. That would go last. We had always known it would be this way, had always known it would not be easy, but the event was now so much more nuanced and so vague all at once, so real as to feel unreal. I joked to Sarah about sitting on a chair and looking down at her on the floor. I reminded her I had never been a hugger and didn't intend to get down and hug her even now. Sarah nodded, and chuckled. Catherine, so different, was on the floor holding her hand, bending her ear close to hear Sarah's sometimes whispered words.

After a bit, I asked about whether she wanted us to complete the book we had worked on together. Her quiet, but resolute reply: "By all means." I am a bit ashamed to say that I felt a rush of relief: I felt forgiven for all the times I had failed to be there, to record a thought or offer an idea, the times I had been tired. These last weeks I had vacationed and stayed away to rest. Then it hit me yet again in that moment that Sarah was *dying*—I needed to pay attention to her rather than attending to my own unceasing, internal conversation of distraction. My mind kept wandering inward as a way to keep the emotions at bay. I have never been a person to tolerate much in the way of my own visible feelings, though I can hold others in theirs. Thankfully, Catherine was different—in body and soul. We were a good balancing act.

Then, Sarah's best friend since childhood, who had called her every day for the last years of her life and had walked every step of the disease with her, came in and knelt at her side as Catherine and I drew back to give her room. Sarah whimpered what she meant as a great, happy greeting, and turned toward her dear friend. "I am so proud of you," her friend said. "You are doing just what you wanted to do. You are *doing it on your own terms.* I will miss you so much! But it's time, as you said. So, go, let go." All the while she cried softly and smiled, and Sarah did as well. It felt as if the flag were passing by in a victory parade after a terrible war.

"Sarah is holding court," Catherine observed, smiling; a steady stream of grandchildren, friends, caregivers and staff were in and out of her room, and she was greeting them all, or trying to. Sarah loved nothing more than to be in the middle of things, of people, especially ones who loved her. Perhaps most of us love to feel loved, but Sarah loved being in a *group*—especially one that was loving her and one another; she had always wanted to create days when people could love the day, the food, the dancing, the jokes, the overall sense of joy that could come from a gathering. The night before, in the sleep of separation that presages death, she had dreamt she was at a party; in her sleep she had talked and laughed.

She seemed content. It was in a different, deeper way than before, and yet, deep down it was the same Sarah. She was happy that she meant something to these people and had brought them together to hold each other up at the same time.

We went back in to say our final goodbyes, or so we thought. She was quiet, resting. We sat with our eyes closed, in reverie, resting with her. There came a knock at the door. This woman, our dying friend, who a second before had seemed to be breathing with effort and hardly able to move, popped back and called out vigorously in her inimitable sing-song voice, "Come in!" Catherine and I stared at each other and raised our eyebrows. It was as if we were having tea with Sarah and had been expecting a fourth. Catherine shrugged and smiled. "That's Sarah!" We slipped out to make room.

Outside among the waiting and the grieving, the talk, of course, was of Sarah. Everyone was there, and Sarah was in each of us. We marveled and laughed at her incredible vitality, even in the advanced stages of her disease. Sarah could wear anyone out, even toward the end. She certainly hadn't been idle in the last days of her life nor ever before.

We sat in the lounge telling stories among ourselves and devouring delicious sandwiches provided by the staff. A week to the day before she went into the hospital, one of her last beloved private caregivers told us, Sarah had wanted to go to a huge bead show in Richmond. Some of us couldn't imagine making that trip on a good day—all those people, the heat of an August day, the road trip—and we said so. But they had driven the hour and more each way, bought beads, and strung a pearl necklace for a daughter and a bracelet for someone on the staff where Sarah lived, all in the same day.

"Man, she loved good food!" said a social worker whom Sarah had, of course, befriended. She went on: some two weeks earlier, they had eaten huge plates of spaghetti at a place that Sarah had found, finally—the only one within miles "with the right sauce," according to Sarah; "This is a sauce that is almost as good as what I make."

"We ate our whole platefuls and sopped up the sauce with the bread," the friend said. They hadn't just *enjoyed* the food, they had reveled in it, savored it, loved every moment of the whole meal together. "Yep," somebody said when she finished her story. "That's how it was with Sarah." Every meal was an event, a burst of happiness, a celebration. And at the meal's end, always, was Sarah's question: "And what do you have for dessert?" Followed by a lengthy discussion of mousse over chocolate cake; "How many forks? Ice cream? The whipped cream? No, not this time."

Sarah was the complete package, a full and complicated human being as we all are. She was a woman who lived with many emotions—a good number of them deep and powerful. She demanded, assumed, refused to accept "no," got hurt, returned the hurt, and grew angry. She could be passively aggressive, and aggressively passive. Like the rest of us, Sarah had fallen short of her best intentions many times, slipping into judgment and hard feelings and giving back the same pain she felt she had been given over time. We all had suffered her barbs and fired off our own. But she always struggled to get back on the path of kindness and always made others want to join her on that walk. She was hard on those she knew, but she also showed them how to love fiercely, as she did, though her love was not always visible or without a layer of control on top. She had changed, softened over the last year. Forgiveness had seemed to come more easily in the last few months, as if much that once seemed so important had proved not to be.

Now all of her was dying, and we would wrestle for years to come with what she had left us—what parts would surface in memory when we least expected them, what guilt or remorse or regret we would feel again and again, though by the end she would never have wanted us to feel any of it. The anger and confusion that sometimes accompany Parkinson's in its later stages had faded some in the last months; some space had been opening. Strangely, it seemed like Sarah, lying on the bed placed close to the floor, was looking at us all with eyes that saw more than our faces, as if she were seeing *into* us. And that smile, that smile that played about her mouth the whole time, giving the sense that indeed this was the time and it was just fine, and weren't you grand just as you were.

It was time for Catherine and me to go before we stayed

too long—time for the people driving in from New York and points south to have their time, and then for her family to be with her alone until the end. Her closest friend had pulled me aside shortly after she had come from Sarah's room and said with concern; "She needs to be able to get on with the work of dying. She needs to get calm now and let it come. All these people are too much!" I agreed, but we also looked at each other ruefully; Sarah wasn't going to let even one of them down.

Catherine and I stuck our heads in the door to speak for the last time. But Sarah was red in the face, clearly beyond her limits, desperately in need of a rest. Catherine gave a heartfelt but quick goodbye; I gave an equally brief combination goodbye of heartfelt and numb. Goodbye, friend, Goodbye.

Outside the door we said our other goodbyes to the family and took the liberty of saying Sarah might need to rest. After that, we heard nothing until the next morning. I remember little of that night as it passed for me. I understand that during the night in Sarah's mind there was another party. Someone was trying to dance on the table. She sounded happy.

The Sarah we witnessed as she was dying was a Sarah different from the woman of her larger-than-life years, or even the one at her struggling end—but not a diminished one. She was a presence, exuding some kind of wisdom, full of life even as it left her. Maybe that Sarah left her bed and entered our minds in those hours, then passed on. Or maybe not.

Where had she come from? Where was she going? When would she arrive?

**August 11**

Sarah Z. died on a sunny late summer morning, peacefully and with her family. When the word came, I was on my porch; as with any important event I can see it even now. The leathery end-of-summer leaves wore the dark green that comes shortly before they begin to turn. It had been cool in the morning when her breathing had stopped; when I heard the news, the air was warming. By afternoon, as the word went out to everyone, the day had turned humid and the sun shone through a soft haze. At my house, only the leaves tapping in the slight breeze broke the deep quiet of the country. Catherine, miles away, said she had felt a faint shift in the world—in *something*—even before she knew; Sarah had gone and nothing would ever be the same. I imagined all those people Sarah knew—and she knew many—getting the word in a kitchen or a restaurant; on a back porch or a city sidewalk; phones ringing from state to state, forming an informal telephone tree. How many different people in different places would know the news today or tomorrow, and how it would be for them? Sarah was well loved, and now she was really, truly gone.

Every death is unique. Many are painful; some are blessed in many ways that cannot be counted. Sarah's death was her own, with its own paths, barriers, teachings, and losses. Two things were important to Sarah as she was dying, in the last year especially: to live life as best and kindly as she could, and to offer up the story of her ending. It would describe the hard, and the good, too. She had made mistakes. She so wanted to help people face death with more forethought than she had; she wanted them to know when to give up false hopes and look for the real thing that was coming.

# Chapter Two:
# Waking Up

*We are all of us resigned to death: it's life we aren't resigned to.*

Graham Greene, British novelist

Sarah's death came quickly, but it had been a long time coming. She was diagnosed with Parkinson's disease in her early fifties. Parkinson's does not visit one suddenly, like a stroke or heart attack. It has its own timetable. Parkinson's, she would learn, moves only one way: from bad to gradually worse. Sarah was able to fight it for nearly two decades, but then, in a matter of two years, the miracle drugs she had been taking began running out of miracles and her way of life changed greatly. The irony of Parkinson's treatments is that, while they prevent the complete catatonia of an untreated disease, they have their own side effects. They are linked to the dyskinesia we see in Parkinson's patients, and when they finally cease to halt the progress of the disease, they cause terrible withdrawal symptoms, which themselves can be fatal. The Deep Brain Stimulation surgery had reduced the involuntary movements, but it too was offering less relief than it had promised.

Now, her fortunes had seemed to decline almost daily in ways she had not expected, and with ever-gathering speed. Despite her years of thinking she knew what was coming, she found she had not sufficiently prepared for all she would face, nor for her own intimate experience of it. Her devolving circumstances were demeaning and grievous, and she fought them.

As Sarah later saw it, she might have awakened to the inevitability of the end of her life even while she was fighting it. She might have done a bit more growing up before matters turned so dire. Maybe she could have focused on further planning then, as well as working against the odds to stay in the place she always had been, had called her life.

She had of course, done some preparing, but not in much detail. She had done the usual advance medical directive, made her will, and set aside money for care. But she had not anticipated the facts of her coming daily life.

Suddenly, the time for planning had slipped away. Planning was not even relevant anymore, coping was. Coping meant facing many facets of aging. The anti-aging culture in which she lived took her by surprise, though it had been around her all along. Most shockingly, she discovered that others treated weakness—a now insurmountable fact of her life—not with respect or kindness but frustration and anger.

Sarah found that needing help may become not a short-term matter of recovering from a fall or an illness, but a terminal condition. When a person is over seventy, say, that person will be labeled *old*, and with that their status will change completely. Sarah discovered bit by bit that to get the help she increasingly needed, she had to give up almost everything she had thought was important. She had to face weakness, disrespect, and loss of her possessions. Needing help in the social category of aging meant nearly losing the powerful and competent image she had long projected to the world. She had to face a vulnerability she had known only as a child; it had terrified her then as it angered and terrified her now.

To get the help she needed, Sarah had to work within a social system that doesn't offer much beyond family care and institutional care. Both have their own ways of changing one's place in the world; in both cases it is necessary to conform to the needs of the caregiver. When Sarah became a consumer of institutionalized services for the aging, she never expected to have to give up everything she had— a lot, certainly, but not *everything*. Yet as she grew unable to do everything for herself, she found she even had to give up the right to *decide* what she could keep and where she could put it, and what she could do. That felt like robbery— whether by her disease or by those who took care of her. Moving from a home into ever-restricted "levels of care" in facilities was as shameful as having been kicked from a beautiful home to a room in the basement—and she couldn't see why it had been necessary. She felt the loss not just of her favorite possessions and places and her privacy, but also of her friends, her self-respect and the respect of others.

Sarah discovered the rampant and devastating discrimination that comes to the aging, perhaps only peripherally when they are still mobile, but with a vengeance when they really begin to need help. She saw that "seniors" too often are transformed into children who do not hold the promise of growing up. It is important to remember that the last time people were called "seniors" was before they were fully adults, in school.

At first, Sarah wanted this book to warn people of the rude awakenings that would surely come to them, as they had come to her. She figured being realistic would be less painful than being ignorant. Some things were going to be unavoidable, like giving up one's things, leaving one's friends and beloved surroundings, and gradually, one's dreams. If you didn't do this yourself, others would do it for you—a truly belittling experience. There was going to be discrimination, and maybe even maltreatment, or at least negligence. There must be ways to fight this, but she couldn't figure out what they were. Then, after more time passed, she couldn't fight them anyway; she was tired and sick. The book was going to be depressing.

Then she began to see the book she imagined and the lessons she was giving as heading somewhere else, too. A lighter parallel track of development she had not noticed until the other one seemed blocked by a huge freight train, began to run alongside the dark one.

In a wisdom book of ancient China, the *Tao Te Ching*, its author Lao Tzu says; *"If you want to be given everything, give everything up."* Sarah hadn't willingly given up anything in order to get everything; she felt it had been taken from her. But even when that happens, the result can be the same if one is open to it. In fact, only then, at least for some of us, can the many intangibles one longed for steal in, or show how they were there all the time. They might not look like one expected them to, but they are there all the same. This is one of the oldest spiritual teachings in the world; Sarah experienced a version of it for the 21st century. But getting to the point of recognizing and living along that track too was not easy. She wanted to make that clear, too.

As she faced her new, diminished reality, Sarah passed her wakeful nights in a loneliness she could hardly stand. In those growing hours she couldn't fill with visits, her confidence slipped, and her sunny, strong façade had no one to show itself to. She felt tired and afraid and abandoned. Then, parts of herself she had abandoned in childhood— when she had tried to become tough or be the best—began to appear in the spaces in her brain once taken up by ego trips and expectations. No longer pushed down by the demands she had made of herself and others because *those* were now crushed, much of her earliest self reappeared, floating up through the cracks in her adult self-image. Beneath the exterior of a successful businesswoman and a dynamic, intelligent presence known as Sarah Z. had always lain another Sarah—the deeper, more spiritual and more vulnerable self—the one we all tend to lose as we grow into modern adults. Old dreams of what she had wanted to be and really still was, her neglected religious beliefs, even the love that had always eluded her, began to rustle around the edges and make life bearable in the present.

Those long-lost parts of herself didn't eliminate her anger and fear of dying. They didn't make aging—or Sarah—into something wonderful. But bit by bit those nearly forgotten parts of herself, retooled for now, served her well as the light faded. They were her own approach to her religion, a sense of quiet, a lessening of ego and a growing knowledge that she could reach her final goal: to die consciously, kindly and without pain.

As time began to run out, Sarah had learned far more than she had expected to and she was pretty sure, she said, that a lot of it would be news to other people. After all, she had been dying for twenty years and hadn't thought about much she wished she had. Always a person with a strong desire to give and help others, Sarah wanted people to see what could happen—and what they might miss—if they didn't pay careful attention to their aging and dying well before they were old. She wanted people to think about preparing for loss and change of status, and also about accepting changes, however painful. She wanted to show how quietly the peace and recognition beyond success and failure settled in. She wanted to share that, beyond the faceless social system that can grind us up, there are the faces of friends and family. New people show up when others may fall away. At the end, Sarah wanted people to understand that she had still died as herself, with dignity and pride, and that the option was open to all of us.

But to say profound ideas outright is to sound hackneyed and trite, or like a greeting card for the aging. Only if you see the day-to-day of it all in a person's life—from the loss to the understanding, feel the pull of it back and forth, the ups and downs—does any of it change any brain cells. For facts to become bells in some part of the mind that might ring later, they must be told as a human story.

Humans learn most deeply by stories. Our knowledge comes from and is embedded in context. We remember people's stories more than lists. To know the truth of phrases that seem vague from the outside, you need to see how they grow from the inside.

The lessons on aging and loving in this book are thus presented not only as lessons, but as growing out of Sarah's story.

We all are our own people. We will face aging as who we are and with what we have. Maybe you aren't Sarah and wouldn't want to be. But what she can tell might be useful in your own story.

For that to work, it is best to know a little about her, who she was, what she brought to her aging and then her death. However different we are, we are all also the same. Sarah found the wisdom that lies in all of us—through fights, discoveries, fears and all. If we can see ourselves in her, at least a little, we can learn about ourselves and our selves to come.

# Chapter Three:
# Who Was Sarah Z.?

*I have been sad about aging. Not because I have*
*some idealized vision of youth. I never enjoyed youth*
*the way some folks have. I have never been a great*
*athlete or a great beauty or a person of*
*huge unending energy. So, I asked God for the*
*umpteenth time...What can I do with the rest of my*
*life that will have real meaning?*

**Sarah Z.**

To really understand what Sarah discovered, it is useful to
know something about how she handled change and how
her mind worked. It is helpful to see how others saw her and
she saw them and what she most wanted from others and
herself.

Even if you don't particularly care about what Sarah
herself did or felt, seeing choices and regrets through
another's eyes can make it easier to see your own.

About Sarah I can of course only tell you what I know—
what I saw and understood and what she told Catherine and
me as we talked for many months before she died. I learned
from her oldest friends as well, but in truth I only knew
Sarah near the end of her life. I am told she was even more
of a dynamo before I knew her, and overall had been
changed by her disease in ways I was never to understand
fully. So, you have here who she was when she began to face

26

her end time in earnest, when she entered the stage of her aging that changed her to "old," as I knew her.

## The Dynamo

Sarah was a major presence in any room she entered. She came in consciously and purposefully, without a shred of diffidence or hesitation about the steps she took. She expected to be noticed. It wasn't that she demanded attention or consciously drew it to herself; she was just somehow worthy of it. People gave it to her. She strode into a room wielding her magnificent red, wheeled walker–called a rollator–taking it around turns like a race car or a pair of skis. She was tall and stood tall. She looked at people with a combination of complete confidence and great empathy. When Sarah talked, what she said made sense, even when her voice wavered or her head twitched with tremors. And in those steely eyes there was always both challenge and love, a sense of power but also compassion. Whatever the topic, there was always an expectation that Sarah was due a response–even when she never actually demanded it outright. It was just somehow, well, *clear*.

She had been dealing with Parkinson's for two decades, but Sarah had still run a business, consulting with top echelons of corporate management in the competitive, controversial field of equity training. She had stood up to the best and had more than held her own. She was a successful businesswoman with a conscience who wrote and implemented training programs for Fortune 500 companies. All of that shaped who she was, whatever happened.

Sarah made it clear every time she said anything at all that, to her, life was worth thinking about and fighting for. Living was good, but there were also the *how*, and the *why*, and the actions you took to give that life meaning. It wasn't only her *life* Sarah fought for; it was the right and means to be someone of value to others, and someone who would be seen and known for what she did and who she was. She was proud in the best sense of that word—pride meaning authority and self-respect. She wanted to fight for other people's pride too; it is why she had made a career in the field of diversity. Sarah believed no one should die without dignity and personal authority; she was willing to expose her own mistakes and discoveries for the sake of others who would follow. Until the very end, she wanted to contribute to the social good.

As she grew ever more tired and felt less able, the rollator became essential for short distances, but Sarah went everywhere even so. Parkinson's changed her gait, but she kept her back straight as a drill sergeant's and was just as focused. She kept moving—fast. In her presence that rollator often seemed to vanish altogether. In many of my memories she stood upright on her own.

Sometimes her rollator turned into a Willys Jeep from an old war movie, with Sarah the classy woman officer in bright red lipstick reviewing the troops, saluting the soldiers— who always saluted her first.

A friend once wrote a poem that Sarah kept in her notebook, about a quiet companion who went everywhere with her. Perhaps her companion never had much to say and never ate much at the restaurants they frequented, but the companion never strayed so far that she couldn't be there in a second or two for Sarah. Only in the last line did the poet-friend mention Sarah's companion by name: "Harriet the Chariot"—her red rollator. And so the rollator was known. Sarah loved that poem; "Oh, have you heard the poem my friend wrote?" She would open the notebook and read it aloud again, as if for the first time. I think back to how it must have been when she first had to bring Harriet into her life, a while before I knew her. Her first steps with Harriet must have been a painful and visible sign of what was ahead. But Harriet—well, she was a *chariot*, and there was nothing weak about that.

Though it was difficult for her friends and family to accept, Sarah was more interested in her personal freedom to do as she thought and knew she probably could, than she was in "keeping safe." What was the point of keeping safe if it meant you lived as half a person, or someone you weren't? Wouldn't it be better just to fall down and die while you were at it? But of course, it wasn't that easy. Just because you fell, didn't mean you died. You just became someone else's problem, and she would *not* be that. So, she settled for help when she needed it, for "care" to keep her free but safe. When she needed more help to do the basics, it was because she needed to keep her freedom. She thought the care would help her do that. That it did in some ways, but in many did not, was one of Sarah's rudest awakenings in the time

I knew her.

## Exuberance

Sarah loved to eat, but only good food. Anything less in a restaurant she would point out, and see that it was set right for her guests. Her own cooking was outstanding and she said so. She loved to make and serve good food—and plenty of it. When she later found herself in institutions with set meals of a middling level, she would often find it insulting, even demoralizing, to face a plate of items that were often cold, perhaps congealed, and overall the product of a system that clearly didn't care what it "fed" to people. If she was paying for good silverware and cloth napkins, she expected the food and service to match.

When she had to move to smaller places as her care needs increased, the food and service, in her view, worsened. Her assigned tablemates, unlike Sarah, often could not read the menu nor remember what it said; the staff treated them impatiently. She found their treatment angering and painful. Rather than face that some days, Sarah would make some strange concoction in her microwave—usually involving tomato sauce it seemed—or go out with a helper or a friend. Those forays were increasingly harrowing adventures to everyone but Sarah.

She loved the diner, the Chinese place on the corner, and the Mexican taco place with the dusty sombreros and serapes on the walls. She loved the people in these places, the sense of just regular folk—not the pretentious diners who often seemed to inhabit the fancy places, and the falsely fancy ones. She could sniff these out.

Sarah loved to bring people joy, or at least a little levity. An average, humdrum event became a hilarious, double-over-laughing story in her skillful telling. She could time her lines and one-liners like a stand-up comedian at a Borscht Belt resort in the 1950's. Jewish humor was the language of her stories—wonderful, hysterical, barbed, but somehow familial, jovial, kind, and also with a sadder side to it. Her humor was never cruel; it said life could be hard for people, including her. People could become hardened as a result and they would have to work not to be, as she had to. The humor worked, because beneath that sense of humor in Sarah lay a strong vein of the serious and the heartfelt.

It is said that humor is born of suffering, something the Jewish people—Sarah's roots—know well. As Israeli hero Golda Meir said, "Those who don't know how to weep with their whole hearts can't know how to laugh either." Sarah had largely abandoned her Jewish faith during her lifetime, but her Jewish cultural upbringing wound through her like a golden thread. She wept too—especially as she found her heart and faith both growing at the end, as we shall see.

In a nutshell, Sarah was a down-to-earth, hard-driving, thinking person who liked to be treated well, but also had a strong streak of empathy and respect for others. She wanted the same treatment for them, too. Maybe it was the New Yorker in her; she knew what she wanted and made her views clear. She was her own unique self, a character from the big city who had sophistication and brashness, a sense of humor and a voice to be heard over traffic.

In 2017, before I knew her, she wrote about her own exuberance and how she feared it was leaving her.

## Exuberance 7/17

*I know that you're still there, in and around the challenges.*
*I recognized you the moment I looked at*
*your shining face on my card. Come back! I need you!*
*My heart recognizes you and yearns for reunion...*

## Exuberance Answers:

*I am here! Let go of your expectations, hard tho' that will be,*
*and in the absence, the silence, the wonder—I am.*
*You are not alone.*

## Soft Spots and Friends

Thus far, the picture you see of Sarah is one of someone strong and with a clear sense of her own agency. When she could, Sarah could figure out how to get what she needed, even if it meant harassing everyone involved or enrolling new allies until she did. She was someone who saw the world as a challenge, yes, but one she could meet. But she had another side, too. Don't we all?

Most of us try to hide our softness if we can; some just can't. Despite the humor and confidence, Sarah was in-between. She didn't wear her heart on her sleeve, but it wove like the strands of a rope around everything she did, even on the most demanding of days. Her full range of emotions were cabled together—the vulnerable with the dynamism, the exuberance with courage. The latter two protected the softer parts of her, but not always or completely. She could still hurt when the rope was pulled too hard or rubbed the wrong way. I don't know for certain how it was before. But by the time I knew her it seemed that the more vulnerable she became physically, as those dynamic strands became frayed and more easily broken, the heartfelt ones seemed to become more visible. But being more visible, they could also become more raw.

In this culture, and particularly for the aging, tenderness can appear as weakness or quaint. "Such a sweet old lady." For those whose lives or temperaments do not allow them to be weak, they may adopt a persona of great learning, sophistication or privilege to cover or repress their soft spots. Others might manage with a degree of isolation or a gruff exterior. You might have supposed that Sarah could or would use her toughness and glamour to keep her gentler self safe. She did, but not consciously. Something else was more important still.

Sarah had long since found that the best way to manage her tenderness and satisfy her heartfelt needs for a degree of safety as well as acceptance and love was to find people who could give those to her. She would give these back in turn—she was more than prepared to. Cold and distant, she was not. She not only wanted to be and have friends; she wanted others to like her. She loved her family, and wanted to love and be loved by them, at the end perhaps more than ever before.

She felt for people, which meant she drew many to her.

She loved the underdog, the brilliant, the sick, even the forgetful who eventually lived all around her. She sought people out—the different, the interesting, the struggling, and she would give of herself to them. She couldn't abide falsity or pretense, from too-cheery smiles, to falsely friendly greetings or "gentle reminders."

Her egalitarian attitude made for an interesting group of friends and deep relationships—when they could happen. For Sarah was also demanding, not only about her own needs, but about what other people needed to bring to a relationship with her.

She would befriend nearly anyone, but to take someone in close, she had to know the stuff they were made of. She looked for people who wanted to go deep. She would tell almost anything about herself if she thought it might shed light on something important that she wanted to know about life—or draw a laugh. She knew how to ask the hard questions: "What makes you say that? How do you know?" But she asked them with a respect and interest that made many want to answer.

When she moved nearer her children at the end of her life, she left dear friends behind and set out to find new ones. But she wanted her own "peeps," she said, people who could talk seriously and be like the old ones. In this new place, she faced the rude awakening of meeting people with whom she had not grown older. They hadn't aged together. These people seemed different. A bit snooty, even, or vacuous, or clueless.

But *really*, she said, how could people with Parkinson's or who were clearly getting old say they were fine and ask you how you were, when you knew for a *fact* they must be scared to death of dying, and usually didn't give a tinker's damn about how you were? What were these people thinking, who exercised like crazy and ate only nuts and fruits because they thought they could age gracefully? There was nothing graceful about aging! Why didn't people talk about grief and loss and what it felt like to lose yourself or another to some illness? What about dementia? Instead, she said, it seemed the closer people got to the reality of dying, the more they tried to deny it all. Back from a Parkinson's support group, she was depressed. It wasn't her thing—it completely missed the point of a support group. "The women were asking how much longer their husbands could live," she said, "and how they could keep them going. That's what they asked!" As she saw it, "They were all about keeping their man around— not about what was happening to him."

It was hard to make friends when the side of herself full of judgment kept cropping up. It was painful and lonely for Sarah not to find friends, people she could be with, and yet it seemed the acceptable fish in the pond were not as many as she had hoped. Some came and went, overpowered perhaps, or uncomfortable. Perhaps she had always had difficulty with being choosy and still needing lots of friends, but now the time to work on making friends was less.

But did I detect an edge? A bit more brittleness, borne of her own knowledge of how death must be done alone—

which could not yet sit well with her? How could a person who needed other people in order to be her full self, to feel alive and safe, face dying without them? They wanted to believe they weren't aging like she was but she knew they were. Could she see why they acted as they did? Did she also feel afraid? Well, if she couldn't have deep friends, she would need more friends with whom she could at least keep busy.

To drown out the low sounds of death and the slowing down of her own body rhythms, Sarah liked to have something to do all day, every day. Especially as matters worsened, she needed to be taken out of herself and her own loneliness. This caused another difficulty for new and would-be friends, especially the younger ones she found more to her liking; she was physically demanding of them. They had to be smart, but also available as much as possible, which often meant a lot. Those with their own lives still out on the track going round and round couldn't afford the time, or couldn't find the energy, to be what Sarah wanted.

So, she recruited more friends, importuned her family, and even invited herself places. She was always ready to flip open her calendar and ask when she would next see you or me for lunch or dinner, or to visit your farm or go to the beach, though she was willing to set the dates a few weeks or even months into the future.

Still, Sundays proved to be sacrosanct to nearly everyone. She so wished she had her own someone, and she still looked, but she knew it wasn't going to be, so there she was.

She said she spent those days alone in the tomb-like quiet of wherever she was living, especially assisted living, until someone she had arranged for showed up to read to her or teach her Hebrew.

When friends came or she went to see them, her intensity and seeming indefatigability (though this was more and more a matter of will) could wear them out. She even frightened them as she began to seem always about to fall, despite Harriet. She never felt she would and made them rush with her around stores and along sidewalks for a turn in the fresh air. She could not understand others' needs sometimes to be afraid for her. She could not understand why a pair of cowboy boots might not be a good thing now for a round of square dancing. Why wouldn't I take her to the boot store to get some? Should I say to her it was because I was afraid she would break something? Shove her disability in her face? But there I was, trying to keep her safe, rather than respecting her wishes. Well, that hurt her, I know. And it hurt me too, in a different way.

Of course, Sarah got angry when she was hurt, as we all can. It just seemed to happen too often, at least in the last years of her illness. It could be hard sometimes to tell exactly what lay under the visible anger, or the passive aggressive form it took. Sarah was skilled at that. She could shut down a conversation with a quick, biting round of, "It's really fine, I'll be fine. I didn't mean to bother you." At the end of her life, she seemed to feel this less or controlled it more; the anger came and went more quickly, and the passive aggressive turned into forgiveness and understanding sooner than it had before.

Perhaps because life itself had shown her the true meaning of rejection—life itself was going away and her body and medications were betraying her—near the end she seemed to take any everyday, unintended affront more gently. It seemed that the phone calls were less fraught near the end. I think she understood that those who seemed unable to give as much as or just what she needed—like me—were still there, still worth knowing and loving for who we were. But getting there took accepting not only the foibles of others, but some old desires lodged deep in herself.

Sarah was nothing if not complex. She had boundless generosity and kindness, and resources to give to those who needed them. She took the time to be kind. She was compassionate and passionate. She looked for what people needed and tried to give it. This was about more than wanting friends; it was about her truly caring—about justice, sadness, needing, wanting. She knew what these were. She would study a person and offer advice so deeply considered and gently delivered that it made sense. When people could see how this side of Sarah balanced the harder, more brittle side, as it always did, it is easy to see why those who stuck with her did so.

Sarah loved art and loved to buy it from anyone who dreamed of beauty and honesty and could make it into form. The person and the work mattered much more than the name. At the end she gave away much of her art; one felt she was giving a little piece of her heart. She made her own wearable art—elaborate necklaces of semi-precious stones— and taught others how to make them. She offered them as gifts, even up to the last week of her life. She loved to give people something she had done especially for them— a card, a meal, a bit of jewelry, a party.

Most of all, Sarah loved parties. She could be her most social self then, friends everywhere, lots of talking. Jokes and stories. She could dress to the nines, show off her latest companion, and feed people. Even as those options narrowed, she still loved to get people together. She loved to plan and celebrate her birthday, though by the time I knew her, the insecure side her of worried and dreamed that no one would come (of course they did). On a card for Sarah's 73rd, and last, birthday, featuring a dozen smiling women in vintage bathing suits, arms locked, marching toward the camera, a friend's inscription read; "You seem to attract a clan wherever you go."

She also liked parties because of another side of that softer, compassionate side of herself as well; she was a networker. She wanted people to meet each other and make alliances that would make the world better—to enjoy one other and become friends. She wanted that; didn't everyone else? She figured they must. It was nothing special. Later she would discover it was a great gift in a country of strangers.

### Courage

Sarah was brave; she must have been to work in the heated professional field she chose. Rather than heading into denial now, most of the time as she approached death, she kept doing her best to observe the process. She fought what she didn't like, or found wrong, or hurt her. It took her a while to realize that her days of fighting were coming to an end, but she looked at that, too. When she grasped how reality was weakening her abilities, she would say; "I think that needs to go in the book...make sure you get that."

Perhaps because she had known about her end state with Parkinson's and her death for a long time, I never saw Sarah afraid of death, only of the pain she imagined would come and the shame that would be associated with the disease's version of it. Parkinson's disease, left to play itself out, would slowly rob her of all vitality and bodily control, and would offer its own kind of dementia. She knew that it would do this, but not kill. She was deeply worried about how this would all end, and she talked about it.

Even so, Sarah was also human, and after a bout of looking her ending in the face she would drop the subject. She had plenty of dreams about a new and better place to live in the meantime to keep her busy. This was courageous or brave too; despite the hard road and the frightening end, she would keep going, keep looking for the "next best thing." She would not stay in places that did not respect her or the people around her; time was too short.

She was determined always to keep the Parkinson's at bay for a while longer. She did in fact keep that free self, the dynamo, the clear thinking, going just by sheer will power. She was ready to grab any opportunities that might come by for the improvement of anything from her health to a new living arrangement. When they didn't work, as they never did, or not as she had expected, she quietly dropped the subject. She felt betrayed by the culture of "aging well," the culture of "eldercare," a culture of denial and disrespect of the old, and her own gullibility. Why hadn't she seen this coming, and how had she fallen for all the hype about the "Golden Years"? Instead, she was facing the eroding of her personal power. That takes more courage to accept than most of us can muster.

Sarah had gotten this far with her Parkinson's by fighting it; the strategy had worked for twenty-two years. She would continue it. Any problem, from tasteless food to rude staff and ignorant people, even to the Parkinson's itself, was to be solved. Everything wrong could be cast as a problem. When one couldn't be solved now, or well, she pushed on it, then under it, and then around it, and she pushed ahead.

But Sarah's life slope was steepening, and her decline was picking up speed. The body and mind she had fought for all those years began to leave her, and through long, sleepless nights and tired days, she felt the end rumbling toward her. In those times, in ways none of us can really know, she faced the elephant in the room of all our lives, as its shape inexorably became visible. Now, those lofty ideals many of us hold about how we will end quietly in our sleep, kind to the last, became practical issues for Sarah. She was determined to keep her *self* intact, keep being who she was. But how? She wanted to show kindness and love at the end. But could she?

Well, whatever happened, she would fight to keep all the freedom and pride and decency she could. After all, for Sarah, in the end freedom was always about being able to make your own choices, and her choices included those things more than anything else.

Sarah had long ago decided that when the Parkinson's could no longer be controlled, she would figure out how to leave her life in whatever way she could. It was easy to say this; "I'll end it myself before then," she said. But again, the reality wasn't so easy in a culture that was set up to keep the elderly safe even if it took their spirit. It saw those of a certain age as a burden rather than the contributors and competent people they had always been, as Sarah still wanted to be. They surely couldn't contribute to their own death!

How did a person die in these circumstances? Could you at least have a say in it? Did you have to have permission? Who would give it? If you could decide about something— like when—how did you say goodbye and pull the plug on a certain day? When did you know it was indeed time?

The issue for Sarah was not about what might come after death. That would be what it was—there were "no data," so why worry too much about it? It would be clear soon enough. She had to get through now. She said once: "It's not about what lies beyond my furniture; it's about how not to be afraid when I'm sick and dying."

For that, Sarah said she would "live until I'm really done." And she would not die "facing the wall," either that of some last nursing facility, or a metaphorical wall of nowhere else to go. Dying would be her last strike for freedom. She would figure it out. Death would have her body, but it wouldn't have her goodbyes. Determined and more and more comfortable with her decision, she lived until her last day, her pride, dignity and her love all intact and whole. She died in a way that was under her control. In that way, despite all she lost, Sarah never lost control, never admitted she had no choice. Everything else, you see, depended on that, even her required surrenders.

### The Downward/Inward Spiral

The process of aging into the end of her life took Sarah about two years of continuous and difficult change. It is this space—the time between life as it was and life as it became— that is not often discussed or fleshed out at the end of a life. But it is the most important space of all; the move from being an adult to being an old person facing death is not to be devalued but seen as a time in which to ask and answer life's last questions. However it happens, life will be sure to send these questions your way. Whether you pick them up or leave them lie is your choice, but Sarah being Sarah, she always picked them up.

The next chapters will describe how Sarah's strong and complex personality, along with her expectations and dreams, fared in the face of the changes that came to her life as we worked together near the end. But to give a summary of the motion of it now, it's best to say that she went from who she was, to a battle to keep that self, to its near-loss, and then to some place of resolution—sometimes all in the same day or week—and then back again. The spiral was always downward, which blessedly meant also to the place of resolution, because the downward also meant an inward turn, even all the way back to who she had brought into the world at her birth. Fight the lessons of aging and death, and you will not win. But listen and learn, and they will bear you up. Perhaps that was Sarah's most important lesson—to herself and to us.

# Chapter Four:
# Freedom and Surrender

*'Tis the gift to be simple, 'tis the gift to be free,*
*'tis the gift to come down where we ought to be...*
**Shaker Hymn**


*...Simplifying is a survival skill. I've learned to be*
*aware of 'the disease of one more thing...'*
**Katy Butler, The Art of Dying Well**

Aging entails giving up life bit by bit, until the last giving up of life itself. Sarah never thought she would have to simplify her life again and again, even down to a level that generated a gnawing sense of humiliation. But aging does require getting rid of much of what we thought defined us. Maybe we can do this on our own and consciously. That is best. But it is not easy. Who wants to give up what they value—material, personal, or metaphysical? It is easier in the early stages, but aging is an unfolding and unravelling process, and so the surrenders will have to continue until death comes.

No matter who we are or what we most value as we age, one of the biggest things most of us must give up is where we live. This can happen several times, each time and each move requiring the surrender of more space and thus of the keepsakes and mementos that can no longer fit.

Our piano is useless if we can't hear or have forgotten how

to play it—but we may still want to keep it. The favorite chair, desk, or painting finally won't fit in the space we can actually afford, manage, or are given as we near the end, however much they once meant.

Those who decide to move early often say they are looking to cut down the clutter and make life easier—to be free of many chores that have become hard or dangerous. No yard to mow, maybe, or no bushes to trim—no need to paint the upper story of the house on a ladder. It feels good; the new, easier space is freeing. But what begins as a sense of freedom may become a growing sense of loss, as people face the real reason for giving up parts of their lives, which always is because they are no longer able to keep them. Toward the end, more moves will follow, perhaps jarring ones like Sarah's. Then, as what should come as no surprise but does, the process of losing speeds up.

Sarah hadn't expected to lose her strength as quickly as she began to. Yet aging tends to work that way; the progressive dimension of it seems minor at first, with small changes over time and long plateaus before the next appear. But some time later the process speeds up, and the changes come faster with shorter gaps between them. Now more and more, still early on in her final slide, Sarah found that each day she faced new changes in her body which made for new needs, and necessary losses. She had to give up increasing bits of her freedom to meet them. These went from losing the ultimate freedom of driving a car to the intimate freedom of making her own bed. But she didn't know all that yet, not really.

## The Last Moves of a Lifetime

Sarah had lived many years of her adult life in the South,
where she had important work, great friends, a partner, and
a house filled with beautiful things. She had, as we say, a
good life. She was Sarah then, and except for the slowly
advancing shadow of Parkinson's, her life felt real and stable.
She knew she would make the move one day from that life
to another, simpler one, but that other one she had already
created in her imagination, in the way everyone does. It
would be happy and even include greater closeness to her
family and old friends. She had not quite anticipated how
her leaving would stir up more complicated feelings than
those in her imagined life, but how could she have known?
It always comes down to that one physical, real day:
the moving truck comes, and the rooms are emptied out as
a life is dismantled. How does one take that last look back?

The truck in this case drove to another city and an
apartment—smaller to her, though it was still large by many
people's standards. It was closer to her family, and some
friends lived only a state away. She thought it would be
liberating, and cozier, with everyone closer. In fact, it was
rather easy to let her other life go, because the story she had
been telling herself up to then was a good one. First, she
would be free of upkeep and the work she could no longer
do at home. For Sarah, freedom was air; and it did feel like
she could breathe better, at first.

Sarah told herself she was leaving to be closer to her

family. But deep down she must have known that she was moving because she and others thought she needed to. She wanted to be freed up to be with her family, and they had asked her to come. But she also must have known that soon she would need them—and they knew that, too.

To her mind, at least as she convinced herself, the move was going to be a turn not away from, but toward, home. It would be a time of sharing wisdom with her grandchildren, taking them to museums and events, explaining what their parents could not. She would go to the family parties and join the holiday dinner table as the queen of a now sizable family. It was going to be wonderful: she imagined herself, as we all might, eventually sitting in a comfortable chair in a family living room dispensing knowledge and wisdom and calm like the grandmother she was. Her presence would be a balm and a joy to her family.

Of course, this placid, intimately involved maternal and grand-maternal woman was someone she had never been, nor would such a domestic persona have suited her for more than five minutes. But when we don't know what's coming, we hang our imaginations on stereotypes and myths, even on characters in TV shows from childhood. Who was she? Opie's Aunt Bea? Those folk-grandmothers who carry giant platters of turkey to the dining table at Thanksgiving? She was more the sardonic English teacher on *Our Miss Brooks*, or the wisecracking Bea Arthur on *Golden Girls*. But she didn't know that yet.

### A Beautiful Apartment

Sarah wanted to be with her family, but she was also Sarah, and so she chose to live in her own apartment with plenty of room for herself. The movers settled her in an airy, spacious apartment in a modern and community-focused complex in her new hometown. It offered neighbors of many ages and nationalities, a lovely clubhouse...and hope. It was pretty enough to feel like home. Sarah was always good at finding friends, or corralling them, and life began to come together again.

She entertained, went to exercise classes, and hosted support groups and meetings. She listened and advised neighbors, like Mary Worth in the funny papers.
The grandmotherly dream now didn't appeal so much.
Her family was close by, and that was a comfort but also enough, for now.

But the slide did not stop. Her growing limitations were manageable so long as she had a housekeeper and driver, which she had been able to arrange. Everyone had those, didn't they? Even people who were doing just fine! But soon she began to have trouble making meals and managing when no one was there. She had to get help for every day. She tried to get a friend or two to live with her full time, but the powerhouse she still was could drain even the hardiest.

### What would be next?

Perhaps she could build a community of her own, with shared help and activities, she thought. It was a lovely dream, and she had had it for a while, but had never acted on it.

Always, everyday life had intervened, and it had seemed something to be done later.

Now, among a few new friends she met around town, many of whom were her age or just a bit younger, she began to float the idea of a place where people who wanted their freedom but also some support could share resources and live together. They would be like-minded, even community-minded, though exactly what that would mean was not clear to anyone—not even to her. She had in mind a house or some other communal space in which people would live as in a real "intentional community," sharing common values, common interests, and common staff—governing themselves rather than being "residents" of an institution. They would eat together, age together, and support one another. They would not be alone and wouldn't need to rely on their families. Yes, the idea of a cozy grandmotherly life had receded in Sarah's mind; she still wanted to be her social, active self.

But the takers were few—not because the idea wasn't a good one, but because it was too hard to conceive, too hard to plan, and too costly for most to embark upon. Maybe if they had begun to plan for it twenty years ago.... And how would it work, exactly? How would they manage when everyone was very old, or someone—or two, or three—got some form of dementia? What if people became very sick? How would new people be encouraged to join so as to take care of the older ones? What about the costs? Sarah's force of personality drove some to research the topic, locate places

purportedly of the ilk but that proved disappointing, and even to visit possible sites with her. They didn't work.
A spiritual focus was considered, and so Sarah got others to study how monasteries and spiritual centers worked. She thought about the results of this research, and then said that while monasteries seemed interesting, she did not really want to live that way because it required a lot of discipline. No one else she was trying to recruit really did either.

Well, maybe they could build a new building! It could have a huge central room, with private suites radiating out from it, and a shared dining room and a nursing wing; they could share the costs of staff and, at least for a while, perform many of the duties like dusting and managing the basics themselves. But the project, as projects often do, got bigger and more complicated and the interest grew smaller.

Finally in a moment of painful clarity that Sarah later related, someone said to her; "Sarah, it's too late for you. There's too much to be done to set up something like this. You don't have the time. You need to be looking for your own place, now, where you can get what you need, and will need." It was hard advice, but she saw the wisdom in it. "In the end," she said, "it came to seem like something we should have thought of sooner."

"Get organized! Plan!" she barked at the rest of us, trying to get us to move on what we still had time to do. But no one really was listening. It was too far in the future, or maybe everyone knew we probably had waited too long already.

Sarah found herself increasingly, heartbreakingly, unable

to function as she once had. She hired full-time help for daytime care and tried to get at least some of her night hours covered. In the last years of her life, Sarah slept less and less; it is a dimension of Parkinson's. Nor were these quiet hours of lying peaceful in the dark. They increasingly were times of nighttime Parkinsonian delusions. She tried to explain that the delusions were more real than the nightmares, or even what was called "reality." She needed people with her to bring her back to an increasingly shaky and unhappy world. Sometimes she got up at night and made her custom cards and jewelry, talked to whomever she had been able to arrange to stay with her, and listened to audio books. She tried not to fall asleep, and not to believe in the crazy and frightening scenes that seemed so real when they came.

During the day, Sarah hid her tiredness and went everywhere. She entertained, took walks with Harriet, exercised, worked on her jewelry, cooked, and more. But now there was always a quiet presence nearby doing much of the work. She made these people friends, but they knew they had a job to do, and the work was hard because Sarah never, ever, stopped.

She remained the force of nature she had always been, setting a grueling agenda of trips to thrift shops and department stores, sending her helpers across town to buy groceries and sundries and later to return whatever didn't quite work, sometimes in the same day or after hours, if she could convince them. She dined out, traveled back and forth to visit with old friends, with the friends driving. She went to her many doctors' appointments, looked at new cabinets, visited with Catherine and me, attended meetings, bought new fixtures for her place, and of course ate out, far more than most of us can imagine doing even for one day.

Even so, the whole thing became more and more difficult for her and those she increasingly needed to help her. She got tired, though she rarely admitted it, and unsteady on her feet, which she also did not admit. Her helpers became caregivers.

Sarah could not abide being alone or without activity, and yet that eventuality seemed to be moving closer, like a tiger stalking prey. Her decline, now mental as well as physical, and her increasing need for help with the many activities she wanted to do or have others do for her, promised that soon much of what she did and lived for would be impossible, and loneliness would find her.

Now the questions were becoming not if, but when. When would she need so much help that she could no longer live alone, even with lots of help? When would she have to stay in a strange place because no one could take care of her 24/7 in her home? When would she need to be cared for by an array of strangers because no one person could manage to care for her? Meanwhile, she was vulnerable to any fall, to her growing nighttime Parkinsonian delusions, and to her own damnable weakness.

So, she took her friend's advice about taking care of herself now and looked for a place where she could keep her freedom by having more people to help her.

To keep that freedom, she would soon understand that

she would have to become more dependent.

She had plenty of money set aside—she just hadn't quite put the financial possibility together with how it would actually look and feel to need help. But she accepted the next dose of reality, set her sights for spaciousness a bit lower, and found places that would suit her, combining at least most of what she loved with what she needed. These were called "senior living" communities.

Today, the pattern of living outside the home that one can expect as one grows less able to care for oneself involves three different levels of care: independent living, assisted living, and nursing care. The combination of these three is also available and is known as a continuing care retirement community (CCRC). Each of these, generally, is a for-profit operation with a very small profit margin.

These options may change in the coming years, but for Sarah these were what she had. And whether they become our own options or not, the problems and issues created are the same ones we will discover in whatever settings we find ourselves, as we need what she needed. The questions remain the same: How will I live? Who will I be? How might I change? Will I be seen, known, respected, or possibly even loved? Who will care? Who will know my own grief and happiness, however I may be able to express them then? When will *then* be?

**The Independence That Wasn't**

Could Sarah have moved in with her family now? Would you if you could help it? Perhaps yes. But for Sarah, despite all her needs for assistance, she was still her independent, free self. Much as she had imagined she would be a loving grandmother sitting at the hearthside, it hadn't happened. She would have lost more independence in the midst of her family life, and they would have, too.

She had a choice to make, and for Sarah it could never be in the direction of less freedom; people with the means often decide they will get professional care when they need it rather than "put their families through that." Senior living was where she would go.

The marketing staff at the place she chose did its job well, as they must do everywhere. The beautiful, understanding, professional marketers made her feel welcome; she was ushered about the place, shown the lovely facilities, and overall given a great sense of being cared for, as in a luxury hotel or a cruise ship, rather than being taken care of, as in a facility. Convinced she could keep the independence she craved with the care they could provide, she would begin her sojourn into the world of elder care.

The place she selected indeed had the look of a luxury liner that many of them do, though one headed in the wrong direction, she commented ruefully once she had moved in.

She was going to have more freedom by giving up the basics of her care; the easiest part of her life to let go. Eating in the dining room didn't feel like such a great loss. No cooking for anyone. In independent living, life would be about doing what she wanted and getting the rest of it taken care of, albeit at a substantial cost. Watching out for her well-being in an unobtrusive way would be the job of many people as well as her personal caregivers—should she choose to employ them. She could do what she wanted to do. So she was promised.

Coming in at an "independent living" level of care, people find it hard to see just how much their lives may begin to change from this time forward. In part the changes come because the body will continue to decline; a place can offer a semblance of freedom, but it can't promise eternal life. Aging begins its crisis/plateau pattern sooner or later, but the desire to go somewhere easier is a deep, if subtle sign that this is coming.

'Independent living" is a name for something that is not independent, or it would not need to be called so. It is a softened name for an institution taking on the first, minimal risks of a continually weakening person's care, and helping to alleviate strains on their energy—and also their worries. In our litigious and insurance-conscious society this can only be in exchange for more control over the protected person's self-determination and agency. How else could it be?

This time, the moving truck came again, and Sarah was duly installed in a lovely, high-ceilinged, wood-parquet-floored apartment in independent living, with built-in bookcases and a screened-in balcony. The dining room was all white tablecloths, hotel silver, and china place settings. The food was decent. She would still be independent here in the ways that mattered, she was told. Activities offered by the facility were close and abundant—vans took people to exhibits and plays. People her age were everywhere.

None of these proved to be very thrilling for Sarah. Everyone looked brainy and well-heeled, the kind of people she could make friends with, the marketing staff had said. If only she liked them more. Her other friends were impressed by her digs and dining options and were happy to be invited to lunch or dinner. But for Sarah, it was over the top. Too much glitz and too little reality always made her nervous.

Her orientation session, she wrote in her journal, did not go well:

> Orientation only took about two minutes and all kinds
> of minutiae came flooding in...this is my home now.
> I will make lots of friends here. I'm in independent living
> which means I still have a bit of control if I remember to
> push the contact button before 10:30 a.m. every day.
> I assume this is to prevent me from becoming another
> headline: "Seventy-Two-Year-Old Found Lying on Floor
> Without Aid for Three Days before anyone discovers her.
> She was dehydrated and practically dead before guards
> discovered her during a routine investigation."
> Hahahaha!

But she didn't think it was all that funny. Somehow the spiel about her independence seemed to suggest she was being hemmed in.

Perhaps this was just Sarah, but it's important for anyone

to realize that this moment will come: this time of being a stranger in a place that will keep an eye on you because you are less than you were. Even if it's your children keeping watch in your own home or theirs, freedom will begin to disappear, even in ways it need not. An older person can become a stranger to anyone. The problem, as Sarah saw it, is that if you are old and then "fail one question on the test of life," you are "assumed not to be able to answer any of them."

Sarah knew institutions. She had been in and out of hospitals for two decades. She knew the subtle cues of discrimination. She recognized the very slight change in vocal tone from steady to a kind of singsong pitch, or the glossing over of questions that comes when one is being played to. She was paying attention. She was leery and hard-headed and not likely to go along with anything just because someone else suggested, recommended, encouraged, or required it. She was there for freedom, not control. This was not good news to the people who now felt her life was in their hands—at least for insurance purposes.

## Who Are These People?

When she shut the door to her apartment for the first time and headed to the gorgeous dining room, Sarah went on full alert. Walking alongside her new neighbors and into the dining room with them, Sarah said, she felt a decided chill. Something about the people felt phony or at least foreign to her. Everyone seemed so gay and engaged; wine was being poured, the walkers were set aside. Waiters buzzed about in white shirts and ties and black pants. What...were people here fooling themselves about the future? Didn't they know why they were here? Or was the gaiety overdone, the laughter a little too shrill?

Sarah was and had been an astute observer in both personal and professional settings. Almost immediately, she found what she believed to be the source of peoples' distance and fear: underneath all the cheerfulness in the room was a dread of dying. Many of her dinner companions, she felt, were strenuously avoiding admitting what they could see more in new people—like herself—than in the friends who were declining at a similar rate as they. It was as though suddenly they had an old person in their midst, and it was she.

The end of the road wasn't real to them yet, Sarah thought, just its next downslope. Besides independent living options, they knew there were other levels of care, not as nice and much more in-your-face about what was happening, but it seemed to her that they pretended these didn't exist. They knew about assisted living and nursing homes, but she sensed they did not want to imagine either. Many of them probably even imagined that by the time they needed such ignominious levels of care they would be too old and perhaps too unaware to care. Of friends who had moved to such levels of care, they rarely spoke.

### A Big Mistake?

Over the next weeks, Sarah became afraid she had made a big mistake. "You'll get used to it; you'll make some friends," administrators said, as if she were in summer camp. The friendly marketing staff encouraged her to take some time to adjust, as they slowly began to let her go, as a car salesman does when he hands you over to the service department.

It wasn't happening. This place to which Sarah had moved, seemingly enriching and promoting independence, lovely on the surface, felt to Sarah to be peopled by quiet, private, or even rude people with their own thoughts and friends. They were working hard to be what they no longer were. She felt she knew what was happening to her and that scared her to death.

Maybe it's common to feel out of place and judgmental when new at a place so different and so seemingly final. But that doesn't necessarily make it easier. How do you live with being told the reality about you is one thing, but having the growing suspicion that the truth is the opposite?

Sarah was sure she wasn't the only person who felt the way she did. She would find others. If no one wanted to talk about what was coming, she would. She was sure some people must be thinking about dying somewhere in those minds of theirs. It likely was all very hard to imagine while you were still dining with white tablecloths and wine. But Sarah assumed that at least a few people must want to wake up.

Well, she thought, they just don't have anyone to pull them together—the ones who think about things, who aren't afraid to discuss how we should prepare for the future, how we feel about what we've lost, and what it has meant to make

this transition. What do we hope for? What's still great?
She would do what she loved to do and pull them together.
She loved to host events, feed people, have good discussions,
and all that. Why not do it here? She had read a book on
aging and transitions. These were transitions, for sure.
So why not start with that?

Sarah took much of the preparation in hand herself.
She put up a flyer inviting people to a discussion of what
she thought must be of interest to all: issues and experiences
of aging and transitions:

**New Here?**

> **Looking for more/deeper friendships?**
>
> **Interested in graceful/wise aging?**
>
> **Interested in developing a small group of friends
> (men and women) who see one another weekly to
> play, learn and become a deepening source of
> support as we approach the challenge of aging?**

Sarah had included her phone number. No one
responded. Not one. No one even called to inquire. It
disturbed and hurt Sarah greatly. What was wrong with
them? What kind of place was this? Why was no one even
admitting there was a huge elephant in the living room?

Denial has its drawbacks; mostly that choice will
eventually be someone else's business and you will be not a
person but a problem. But to choose the opposite is painful.
It requires difficult days and wakeful nights of thought and

conversation, reading, returning to spiritual roots, and much more, all a kind of anticipatory grieving.

## Going Down

Whatever she thought of others or believed of herself, Sarah was slipping and growing weaker. She was unable to do much. She fell and needed nursing care for a few weeks. She realized that yet another surrender—past independent living—was gathering like quicksand around her waist. Life was coming to be less about living well, and more and more about just living.

Sarah wanted to keep the self-respect and the respect of others she had fought her whole life to attain. In her journal she wrote; "I will of course die, but I had hoped to have a modicum of dignity left by then...." Thinking that it might not happen that way she wrote: "This seems to be a tough lesson for me." She wasn't sure how to hang onto that dignity much longer.

## Another Move?

Frustratingly, frighteningly, and sadly, it began to seem that Sarah had made her move to independent living a little too late. She began to need help around the clock, and this help was hard to come by. It could only be brought in; her independent living apartment did not offer personal help beyond ensuring she was alive every day, not in need of emergency care, and was provided a safe community. It did not offer direct care, nor personal assistance. More and more, what she did involved the logistics of getting seated in a car and getting out, stepping up on curbs, going over bumpy sidewalks, avoiding the danger of falling, and dealing with confusion.

Others of some authority in her independent living community—always cheerful, always in dapper suits and high heels, always deferentially calling her by her formal name—began to discuss with her that it was growing very difficult to keep her safe in her apartment. It was just, well, hard for her. And indeed, it was.

Sarah began to see the danger herself. She was still increasingly afraid of falling, having done it and ending up bedridden and in nursing care for a time. It could easily happen again. At night she might get lost in the ample space of her apartment and fall there or become disoriented and not able to get back to bed. Her friends, and the night caregivers she had hired, tended to fall asleep on the sofa. She needed to feel safe while she slept or tried to, and it was becoming ever clearer that she needed increasing support just to get through the day. For all of that, she needed more care from more people who would observe her more; that way, she thought, she would still be free because her limitations would be handled by others. She only vaguely sensed that help would necessarily take away more of her freedom in the name of care.

### Time to Move Again

It was time to move again, then, to assisted living, and so she picked a place she thought would be tolerable and made the move. Downsizing yet again, this time to fit into an assisted living apartment, meant surrendering even more of her precious belongings than she had already. In fact this time, it was nearly all of them. Many of her remaining things, her beloved outward symbols of her taste and flamboyance, were to be traded for safety. To the degree her own sense of herself was tied to her things, she was losing that, too.

The nice administrative staff members in the place she chose told her that there, she would get the support she needed to remain as free as she could be. They were indeed kind, and she was indeed her determined, not to say demanding, self as she tested them. She wanted a unit like this or that. Now, not later. With a better view. Bigger. A different layout. Were they really all the same? Could she go back to where she had lived before if she didn't like it? How could she? That place would be gone.

**The Assisted Living World**

The new facility looked okay. The common rooms were nice, but quite a bit smaller than in her independent living facility. It was strange no one was ever in them, but at least the giant televisions in each one weren't always blaring as they were in other facilities she had seen. The nurses' stations on the halls would guarantee she was safe. Should she get confused, they would be there to help, night and day. But nurses' stations! What was becoming of her?

Everything she wanted was promised, or someone promised to "look into it." A pole for balancing upon rising

64

from the bed. Someone to hang her wall decorations. A rack or closet insert. A this, a that. All would be provided. Sarah knew the places were smaller, but she would reclaim some control: she would have all the changes she wanted made to the space she would have to inhabit. The changes were promised not only because it was part of getting people into a place they really did not want to go, but also because people—staff—liked to help Sarah. She could be demanding, but in her essence she was kind, and many of them knew that. Even so, it was difficult for her to see how her negotiations might be in vain, especially when her needs were unique and not according to standard procedure.

Finally, the move came. This time a moving truck was not needed to take what was left of her things. She corralled her caregiver and me to do much of that work on one day: the vase on the porch with giant fronds; the antique mirror; the statues, the giant painting of balloons, papers, the computer, lamps, decorative bowls, couch pillows, all travelled with us. It felt unnecessary to hire professional movers, she said, particularly when she cited the cost. But this was Sarah, not a college student. I broke a mirror and a light fixture; I spilled the fronds. But those precious items we carried were all the intimate bits of her that were left; the few large items that remained—the television, the couch, the bed and some other odds and ends—would fit into a pickup truck. The big-time moving was over.

"Welcome home. You'll be at home here. We're like family," the person in charge said. Susan thought perhaps her fellow residents would be less afraid here; at least they had accepted that they were no longer able to manage alone. Perhaps there would be less of that haughtiness and more people who knew what she knew about life and how it could be hard.

The unit she chose—because she wanted at least an alcove for her bed and wanted it immediately—was not to her satisfaction the moment she put the first stick of furniture in it. Why hadn't she seen it before? It was dark, the carpet a dull industrial brown, the lights garish, and the only view from the two-seater couch (which fit on one wall only) was the kitchen area, if it could be called that. The underbelly of the sink was open to view, with the drain pipes the point of focus. Sarah's sense of aesthetics was outraged.

As all her belongings that she had not been able to leave behind made it to her new place, the place came close to resembling the home of a hoarder. She could barely move around, and her guests could do so only one at a time. No matter how hard and how many things she pushed and shoved, shelved, hung, and mounted, no matter how many closet inserts or storage units she had put in, the place still felt like a second class stateroom on an old ocean liner, without any pretense of luxury. She was trying to get some 1,500 square feet—perhaps more—of stuff into less than 300, including the bathroom, which was the biggest room in the place to accommodate the wheelchair, that it is assumed all residents in assisted living will soon need.

So what? you might say. She had a place to live, and

everybody has to give up stuff. She was lucky to have stuff to give up! This is easy to say, except when it is your stuff. For some, objects hold much of a person's memories and personality. Even if the stash is small, there usually is a photograph, a child's toy, or perhaps a set of beads that is loved until close to the end. For many of us, our things are part of us, and our lives are reflected in them. Only as life leaves does it seem like the objects lose their value to us.

Sarah not only gave up her things and the look of a real home, but she also had to alter many of her routines to meet the routine of the place. Everyone has routines. Maybe it's reading in the morning, or sleeping in, or cooking, or talking on the phone. Maybe it's taking a walk outside. These all get hard to continue in assisted living, especially as the eyes fail and the stove is gone, and breakfast is served at 7:00 sharp, meds delivered at 10:00 and 2:00, cleaning done at 11:00. And how could she live even a little in this space? How could she make her jewelry in this dingy place with no surfaces big enough to work on, and the lighting either harsh or dim? How could she make her cards, or offer someone a bite to eat? Sitting there looking at the pipes under the sink and some groceries that fit nowhere else— forget it. I don't think we ever saw Sarah sit on her couch.

She did not like ostentation, but this place was at the other end of the spectrum. She now had tipped over her limit. It felt humiliating and disempowering, both in how it looked and how, she came to know very quickly, she was treated. Sarah would not take this lying down, even if she had to lie down more often now than she ever had.

No one had hidden these rooms from Sarah. She had picked this particular room, and had known its size. But she was surprised at how the whole thing made her feel, how angry she was, how much it mattered that she lived in less than an efficiency apartment, no matter how classy and shiny the exterior structure, or how nice the halls outside her door.

Sarah railed against the new, cramped, unattractive, unappealing, more suffocating existence that she couldn't believe she had chosen. It seemed cleaning hallways with large machines went on most of the day, medication carts were always trundling about, and the aides at the nurses' station were overwhelmed and often in others' rooms when you needed them in yours. Nurses stood before their medications carts with charts and bubble packs of pills and looked harried and nervous.

There were the occasional lovely lounges that visitors might imagine were common areas where the residents gathered to work on puzzles, to chat, read, play the piano, or watch the gigantic television, but they rarely did any of this. Models were always doing such things in ads for such places, but the real people did not. Once one person entered a lounge, it felt off limits to others. The most familiar visitors were the staff, who stored their lunches in the fridge.

Sarah's sense of loneliness and isolation did not improve in the bare-bones dining room, populated by a few people she felt were in worse shape than she was. They were old;

she felt she was less old rather than ill, diminished by Parkinson's disease. She felt the staff treated them all as if they were a nuisance. It was true, for the most part: the staff who cared for them in their rooms had to double as wait staff; they had trained to be certified nursing assistants, and here they were waiting tables. But it was no fun for the diners either. As Sarah observed in her journal:

> At breakfast in my assisted living we all get up around
> 7:00 and toddle down to breakfast in the small dining
> area that is for our floor and pretty much our floor only
> (although in the Handbook and if you talk to an official
> person it says otherwise). There we are greeted by the
> same people every morning and we are expected to sit in
> the same chairs each day—every meal—and I just love
> doing that parade down the long hallways which
> reminds me so much of the TV show The Walking Dead
> that sometimes I'm chuckling to myself by the time
> I arrive at my table and sit in my very own chair which
> is the same every day for every meal.
>
> This particular morning I am greeted by "Sally," let's
> say, who says "good morning" in that sing-song kinda
> way that people have when they have done a thing a
> million times and they know it by heart.
> "Good morning," I sing back.

But most of all, what Sarah found most inexcusable was the staff's apparent assumption that because she was there, she had lost all ability to judge or make decisions for herself. They couched their concerns, she said, in terms of safety—

even more of a bugaboo here than it had been in her
independent living apartment—and concern for her care:

> They're not interested in anything but safety. Every time
> I say, but why? But why? But why? They'll end up with,
> "It's not safe and it won't be safe. You could fall doing
> that." So, what the f–k, what if I fell? What would that
> be? The end of the world for you? You'd get another
> person coming in who might fall...

> This week it was about pills, who should keep the pills,
> who should have the pills...that was the first half of the
> week. The second half was about my visit summaries
> from my doctors. They wanted those, to keep them for
> me.... I said, "What do you do with this stuff? Do you
> make bonfires at the end of every year? I mean, what do
> you use them for?" And they said, "Well, we have to
> have the summaries because we have your pills, and we
> have to know how your doctor wants them..." and on
> and on.

The most enraging irony of such concern for her safety
was that it had always to do with Sarah's dangerous behavior,
not their own. But she was not the only person who could
put her in danger. Whenever Sarah fell, it often took a long
time for anyone to come to help her. When she needed to go
to the bathroom and was unable to get there on her own or
lost herself in the bed and couldn't figure out where her
head was in relation to the headboard, she rang the bell
again and again to no avail. When she was confused about
where she was and appeared in the hall in her nightwear,

she was chastised. She wanted the much-vaunted staff to know that it was no fun for her, either—that she wasn't stupid or dotty, but plagued by specific dimensions of her disease. The nighttime Parkinsonian delusions, the ones more real than the facts of her room and where the door actually was, were worsening and mercilessly disrupting her sleep. Didn't they get that?

Sarah complained, but it seemed to do little good. She heard from other residents that she shouldn't complain, or the staff would be less inclined to help her. They told her that a reputation for being demanding or needy would make her a "complainer" to the overtired staff. The woman who cried wolf.

Time managed, food managed, space controlled, movements controlled...even her visitors had to sign in and out. For a woman of independent means, a person used to a life that was her own, how else could that feel from the inside, whatever the goals and efforts of the institution itself? And she was paying for this treatment?

For any of us, wherever we are, our lives at some point may well look as though they need to be managed, however we may feel about that inside—or whether it is even true. What appears to be in our best interests becomes someone else's to decide. No one is allowed not to eat, or to eat only chocolate. No one can be allowed to skip the pills, or bathing. No one can be allowed to fall. These are good rules maybe—or are they? When? How does one prepare to live by them?

Sarah's life threatened to continue in this place, a series of setbacks and rebellions, victories and losses. It was a constant struggle to keep what little territory she had left. How could she live in this hole for years?

Maybe the place itself would make her weaker. She would not die a trembling shadow in this cold place without control of her mind or body, completely at the mercy of people, the majority of whom, she believed, did not care who she was or who was in the room she presently occupied. She would not become completely dependent on others. She would get out before then.

## "I'll Fly Away," or Hospice

Thinking of the next best thing, Sarah tried to figure her way out of the mess she felt she had fallen into. She came up with two solutions. The first was to change where she lived altogether, going somewhere that would be truly safe and simple and with nicer people—most likely another assisted living residence somewhere else in town. Getting her own apartment was also an idea and hiring around-the-clock care to take care of her there sounded great. Whatever it was, it had to be nicer and would give her more freedom than this.

The second solution was to change her status from the newly assigned term "aging" to the somehow strangely more dramatic, and socially more acceptable term, "dying."

Unable to keep up the effort of being independent and having to resign herself to assisted living, Sarah firmly decided at least to declare herself "dying." Right now, she couldn't change where she lived—it was too much work, and she might not get her large deposit back—but she could change her label. She might have to live in a dungeon, but she needn't live there long. And she would get the additional, generous care hospice gave brave persons facing life's last challenge.

Hospice accepted only people who had a prognosis of death within six months. Sarah somehow convinced the local hospice officials and herself that she would be gone in six months, or at most, a year. To her friends, she seemed much too full of life still, and they tried to wrap their minds around how Parkinson's might work mysteriously in ways they didn't know. In general, Parkinson's was assumed to be unpredictable and not even fatal (opportunistic events take the sufferer as they weaken), and so it was difficult to enter hospice with that diagnosis under any conditions. How had Sarah managed it? Perhaps because she was Sarah: persuasive, charming, clear-headed, unable to take "no" for an answer. And now she believed she would be dead in a year, after all. Maybe sooner.

The hospice people were wonderfully attentive; a nurse, a social worker, and new equipment and supplies arrived. Still not thinking clearly about what dying would entail perhaps, she felt better; she could stand anything for six months, even for a year.

But hospice could not help her die; it could only help her not to fall prey to those who might force her to live by using invasive therapies she did not want. And of course, they could not support her in anything that might be curative. Did she really want to die after all? Death was a terminal decision. While Parkinson's might continue its downward spiral, the strength remained in her body and her mind was relatively clear. Hospice began to look like a brake on her life rather than a lively option.

In the meantime, as can often happen with hospice, she actually improved somewhat. In trying to shorten her stay in this place she was apparently lengthening it. Perhaps they would "graduate" her from hospice if she did not die within the approved timeframe, and she would still be here! She could be released from hospice now and save it for later, but she was concerned that getting back on would be a little tricky, now that she was proving to be rather chipper.

Hospice or no, and much to her chagrin and pain, it was appearing that she might have to live in assisted living much longer than she had hoped.

The hospice option indeed fell apart after a time. Hospice was about dying, and Sarah began to show signs of wanting to live. She wanted to consider curative care for a problem unrelated to the Parkinson's. That was not the point of hospice. She could return, they said. She could not appeal their decision. Now there it was; she was not going to die. Well, not really, but the set time, the extra care, the hospice identity, the visits from nurses and social workers, were gone for now. It was not only deflating; it was embarrassing.

Sarah continued to rebel and argue against the limitations of the facility. But slowly she had to face the fact that much of what the place was seemingly taking away she had indeed lost. Her body and mind were losing them for her. She couldn't always stay regular with her pills. She needed help, and if the staff were slow in giving it, she still couldn't live without it.

What she had thought of as freeing had always in fact involved a surrender. And the surrender came because her life truly was devolving beyond her control. As she observed, "What's deadly about this place: Here you lose your personal power." That phrase had multiple meanings.

# Chapter Five:
# Respect and Relevance

*Emphasizing the declines of aging and pathologizing life's normal progression...creates disabilities where there might be only differences.*

**Louise Aronson, Elderhood**

When Sarah moved to her retirement community, she soon found that it couldn't be her home as she had imagined it might be. When she moved into assisted living, she was further disabused of the notion that this place, though theoretically designed for people with her needs and given over to their care, would ever be her home.

Neither of these was like the homes she had made for herself in adulthood. Perhaps assisted living resembled the home of her childhood. There she had felt trapped, without status, without a voice, and unable to leave. Now she felt that in this new "home," matters had shifted from giving her assistance to maintaining control—as if she had gone back in time. Again, she was assumed to be relatively useless, not only to herself, but to others. She was to be entertained or ignored, but not expected to contribute meaningfully. To Sarah, everyone like her in her new place was treated that way also.

## Suddenly Old

Sarah had lived with Parkinson's for a long time, but she hadn't been "old." When she moved into this retirement community, she had become "old" almost overnight. She had not expected this new label.

If you are ill in the "outside world," even when you have lived with an illness for a time, you don't become an old person automatically. It is still assumed that you can think for yourself. But being a little past her prime, weakening, and in a home for the retired, Sarah was suddenly assumed to need help not because she was ill, but because she was *old*, which the rest of the world often considers unfortunate, vexing, or unforgivable. She was assumed to have certain *needs* rather than *abilities*. What she could do was ignored or devalued; what she could not do determined her increasingly declining worth. Assumptions were made about what she would want to do, and what she was able to do. Life would be "fun" and "enriching," rather than productive, as if she had no desire to be competent and capable of giving to others. Or was it that no one wanted her skills and gifts anymore?

This view of people, of the old, often called a "deficit model," is commonly held by those with prejudicial views of disenfranchised groups. Usually added to these views are assumptions that old people as they age need to be kept busy and alert by playing games; are happy to watch television; like (and need) to be treated like children; tend to exaggerate their needs; and often are forgetful and querulous.

"Protection" in her mind was a code word for disempowerment. Women, especially, have long been the victims of such protection; older women even more so. Sarah lived in a place determined to keep her safe and occupied, if possible, but what did that mean? She wondered whether her protection and all her supposed "deficits" in this facility were more about keeping her easier to manage than about her safety—more about keeping her powerless than content.

To Sarah, this was no small matter: she felt being relegated to the category of "old" took away basic human rights. The issue of who owned her life and decided what she needed slowly grew in her mind from a personal to a political one. She began to see it all around her—not just in her own relatively privileged situation where money at least created a gilded cage—but in how the aging were treated everywhere, which was usually much worse than she was.

Having spent years as a diversity trainer and advisor to organizations, Sarah saw all the familiar signs of prejudice she had taught about: its labels, its ability to make whole segments of a society vanish into poverty, institutions, or isolation, and its ways of separating people on both sides from their better nature. Whatever the answers, these questions and the conditions that had raised them in her mind were Sarah's political awakening into ageism.

### Discrimination and the Loss of Relevance

As a person well versed in the dimensions of prejudice, Sarah saw how people picked up a set of anti-aging values and vibes from the culture at large, and wishing to or not, brought them into facilities like hers. Places like Sarah's could hardly be blamed or faulted for fulfilling a role that apparently was needed; in fact, such places were a blessing.

But their practices supported and reinforced the negative perceptions of the old that run like river currents through the outside world. These currents have come from many places, but mostly from changes in longevity and new cultural attitudes toward death and aging, rapid technological change, shifting economics, and the constant devaluing of what the aging have to offer. What old people come to be afraid of and resist is not necessarily aging, but ageism.

Many of those around Sarah were ninety and more, and some of them indeed could no longer remember their names or remember her from one visit to the next. But they had not always been that way. What if the causal flow went in the opposite direction—what if people weren't cared for because they were old, but old because they were cared for? Was it possible that the labels of "old," and "aging," with their emphasis on what people could no longer do rather what they might do, pushed people into perceived uselessness far too soon? Sarah found herself a case in point. She had much to offer and needed to figure out just what it was, because it could not be what she had done in her prime. But no one would support her in that quest.

Instead, they saw what she was supposed to be: old. Doing normal things would make her unusual or even special: "Those people still heading out to lunch in their eighties—isn't that great? Why is that so great?" Sarah asked. "Shouldn't we be?" So vital and so funny! Dancing, wearing funny t-shirts, even advocating for their rights! Sarah sensed that the positive comments belied a belief that such things were unusual and just a little silly. Why didn't they act their age?

Many still had skills, clarity, and even new wisdom they could offer, but instead, the people around her were offered classes. Talking about being old or imparting discoveries to one another was not very popular, as Sarah had found out. It felt to Sarah like the old had taken on the prejudices leveled at them. Of course, she had too; she wanted to dress like a younger woman, appear as active as possible, and hide her infirmities. She did it not just because she wanted to, but also because she didn't want to appear old. She knew what the label meant.

More and more, the people around Sarah were losing their mental and visual acuity and balance, as she was. Some even had lost memories of long ago. They were losing the ability to take care of their bodies—as was Sarah. Some were deaf or hard of hearing and could not understand staff members' commands and questions. Some grew angry for many reasons, including physical limitations and changes in their brains, and some were demanding like Sarah.

"Write about this!" Sarah directed us several times. She was angry. She felt she was becoming the target of a prejudice that controlled her mind and desires as well as her furniture, her health, and her comings and goings. Somebody had to know just how old people were treated! They needed to understand! No one likes to lose control of their bladder, nor rely on someone else to clean them. But at least, if allowed, that person could still offer, contribute, something to someone else. Not only was she not allowed to be somebody, but she had also become a problem.

If eventually or sooner, the residents seemed to accept their roles as consumers of whatever was offered, they weren't always passive; some did the autumn leaves on a paper plate project because it was still something to keep them awake and with other people. At least they could do *something* creative. But likely the staff did not see the projects that way; they created activities to help people who finally seemed unable or unwilling to do more. Other people did not do these activities, but they then had to sit in their rooms. What could they offer or gain from there? Only kind words and expressions of satisfaction about where they were. It was strangely Kafkaesque. A nurse asked Sarah:

> *"How did you sleep?"*
> *I have a few choices and only those:*
> *"Okay;" "Well, thank you;" or "Fine."*
> *"I'm so glad to hear that," she says.*
> *"Yes, me too," I say.*
> *That's the only way you can answer that question here.*

## Fighting the System

Sarah was not done yet, not by a long shot, she thought. She would keep her power and her dignity. She would contribute to improving the ways people like her were treated. She looked for opportunities to teach or speak out about what was happening to older people. Why couldn't people know what was coming, and decide for themselves how they wanted to live? Why couldn't they be seen as something besides "old," or "seniors," or "elderly," or "frail," or some other terms that made them seem less? She requested a formal response to her complaints about treatment from higher and higher levels of management. She went to the top, and she went with reinforcements—friends from the "outside" who could afford to be even more assertive than she. She made herself known, and she did not back down, for herself or anyone else.

The ways in which the aging are not allowed to contribute or otherwise gain respect are often subtle. In Sarah's case, "no's" were rarely given. Most of her requests were answered with; "We will certainly look into it for you." This useful phrase, despite her disbelief in its veracity, always made her feel better, even though she knew they hoped she would forget. It was what everyone was told, even the once powerful men and women who served on the residents' council. Nothing really had to happen—administrators and staff just had to wait people out; the system and their own failing bodies would grind them down.

Over time, most things Sarah thought of to do to help others or herself died aborning—they remained being "looked into."

Eventually, Sarah wore down too. The whole effort at advocacy began to seem like arguing with a pillow; the sound went in, but nothing came out but solicitous smiles and promises until she pushed too hard. Then she got the treatment of anyone making demands above their station:

she was told that mysterious "reports" on her were not good; she seemed a little "out of control," as anger is often described when it comes from those who have less power than those with whom they are arguing. Again, women know this well. Imagine how it must be for old women, and then old women in a facility built on the premise of their inability to be useful or care for themselves. "Why can't she just calm down?"

Rightly or wrongly, Sarah began to fear that much more of her demanding and angry activity might occasion a dementia label and a move to a memory care facility. This frightened her more than almost anything; the strong woman not afraid of power grew afraid of unseen people in a hierarchy who could change her life with a call to her children and "finding a bed" where she belonged.

Using the deficit model, staff found it easy to label the complaints or irritation of residents as signs of being deficient mentally. This indeed can be the case. But maybe some residents' unhappiness came from a sense that they were not considered full-fledged citizens anymore, and there was no way out. Maybe they had accepted the fact of their powerlessness, and yet deep down that still rankled. Their experiences were very much like those of any population that is the target of prejudice: all their powerlessness was said to be of their own doing.

## Outgunned

Here is a glimpse into how life was for Sarah and others in her circumstances, a combination of infantilization and her inability to fight it. Wouldn't you give up?

The nurse politely said:

> "We'd like to sit down and just chat with you, a little bit, about certain things."
>
> And then I had said: "What certain things would those be?'"
>
> And they said, "Well, hm-m-m-m-m, we'll talk about that."
>
> I said, "Well, you're not going to give me any hint about what this is?"
>
> [Sarah suddenly shouted at us: "THIS I WANT IN THE BOOK, BECAUSE THIS PISSES ME OFF!"]
>
> So they said, "No, we'll talk about it tomorrow. It's only a day away."
>
> So I sang to them. I had to. I couldn't help myself. "It's o-o-only a da-a-y a-a-way!"

Sarah assumed the request would be about something she was to lose. She had tried resisting these requests, couched as discussions, before. But now, she just didn't care anymore. She would let them win.

She was ready when they returned. It wasn't about the pills, but the medical records they had discussed before. She gave up asking them why and what for. There were two of them visiting her, including the floor's main official; she knew she was outgunned anyway.

*So I said: "Yup, you can have them all. Here they are. Here you go. What else?" They were so stunned that I actually relinquished them. They were ready for a big, I think, fight.*

For Sarah, the fighting was ending now. There was no point. The person of strength and righteousness her whole life and against many odds–from her difficult childhood to her status as a businesswoman to twenty-three years with Parkinson's disease–was going fast, and was already invisible to many. The last goals, the last angers, the last and often most important discoveries, must be left to die their own deaths.

Sarah had wanted to write an exposè about elder care and start a movement against the disrespect and shabby treatment she saw and knew herself. She had wanted to work for elders' rights as she had fought for equality in the workplace. She wanted older people to be able to contribute as she had fought for others to do the same.

But increasingly she realized that while she might have taken on this matter twenty or even two years ago, it was too late for her now. The wall was too high. Each day she was less able to fight or advocate than the day before. She might still have all the mental chops and abilities to save the world with her ideas and her deep reservoir of desire, but her mind and body were slowly changing the Sarah others saw.

This fight was denied her now. It was autumn, and people were hurrying away from her along the cold sidewalks. They were hurrying away from everyone like her.

## The Point She Had Missed

Here is what Sarah had forgotten or perhaps in her hurry had never known: the old don't contribute what the young do, but it doesn't mean they don't have their own jobs. Nor do these jobs come without some discoveries and self-training. Wisdom isn't a given. While there are no schools, nor even any elders perhaps, to teach what must be learned, there is life. The mind, if it is allowed to, finds its way to a different kind of knowledge with a little help from deep memories and old desires.

For Sarah, as for so many before her and certainly to come, it was time to turn inward to her own care and last lessons. This one had been a hard one, but she had finally gotten it. It was time to be old not in the powerless way the culture demanded, but in the powerful way of the old. Strangely, it would have to start with the powerlessness she felt.

Now she would finally have to open up enough to learn the lesson of how to contribute in a different way. She put it like this:

> So, if I wanted to change something here I couldn't do it from this place I am now [the facility] because you have to always say everything's ok.
>
> Now I understand why people cross by each other in the hall and say they're 'fahn' [fine], because really it's too much work not to be fine. It's too much work to know the reality. And now I feel like, well too bad then, I guess the next person will have to do it, and I don't

*care for thinking like that very much. It's not my natural*
*state. So, I feel sad about that. But you know,*
*I can't be taking on the world.*

*Well, I don't...think I can do any more here...*
*My head is changed already.*

She couldn't change the world's prejudices, she couldn't change her living arrangements, and she couldn't change her disease. She couldn't offer any more what she might have offered even a short time ago. In those long nights of wakefulness when she was warding off the Parkinsonian delusions, she decided to believe in her own skills—what she had left–even if others did not care about them:

*I do beads, I do reading, I do writing, I do all that stuff.*
*I collect my notes for you and it's fine. It's really better.*

That was the first step of turning not into who people thought she was nor staying who she had been, but becoming who she was.

### A Future in the Past

In that empty place of seeing that nothing was working, in the midst of anger fading into a level of hopelessness about her desired situation, Sarah's head, and her hopes, did indeed begin to shift. As she puttered about in the night doing what was real to her and available and meaningful and peaceful, she slowly let go of that driven, adult self.

She became aware of new things that were in fact very old—in her, and in all human lives. Now, through a back door, she was finding out what old people should know and could teach if given the chance. Was it coming too late? Maybe not. There was this book, and there was what she would learn next: another lesson, about how an old person of nearly any age might contribute.

## Old in the Ancient Way

Aging is a time when the brain is changing focus. For important evolutionary reasons, it is lessening its work in rapid-response areas because it is expanding in others, into a slower, deeper, wisdom of long-term memory and a different kind of thinking. Anthropological research in other cultures shows that old people are not supposed to do what younger people do any more than adults are supposed to act like children. The acts of giving and contributing to a society, the acts of living on the part of the old are very different than for adults or the "young," and this is a good thing. They are critical in their own right.

The contributions and work of the old have forever involved offering wisdom and guidance, conveying important family history that gives children of all ages a sense of belonging, recalling and offering the rituals of a family or a faith, and much more. In other words, the old hold the overall values and history of a culture. If they don't take the time to do it, then it doesn't happen. Of course there are historians, philosophers, religious leaders, and many others who explain the world in one way or another. But the old have a different role; they are to work intimately with people's individual problems and struggles, using their own lives as the tools to do so. In many cultures, this role of the old is still important; where it is not, it is clear something is missing. Yes, eventually this work of an aging person is no longer possible, but we must guard against that potential being cut off too soon. In our world, there is little general support for drawing on the knowledge of the old, or even for deepening it.

Contrary to modern folklore, the old aren't naturally wise. They have evolving brain power to use to become wise, but it doesn't come easily. They may need to work at it, and then be urged to share their gifts of wisdom and knowledge. Maybe there need to be cultural institutions and schools for aging, taught by the aged. In other cultures, the aging pass knowledge down to the next group that will age, and to children who will carry that knowledge into their own lives. But if you are sitting in a home that feeds you your pills and sets up bingo in the afternoon when you are in your seventies or eighties or even nineties, this can hardly happen.

When was the last time you asked yourself if God exists, or what humans are here on earth for—and tried to come up with an answer? If people are aware enough to think about it, these questions come back to the aging, and become more important, just as their adult selves are vanishing.

### The Beginning of Wisdom

Now, for Sarah, the early dark afternoons sent her friends home early. The staff with whom she shared the frustrating dynamics of care came in and out; she was called for dinner. She ate and tried to sleep and to keep going. She had accepted that all of this would be her home until she died.

In the other rooms along the corridor outside her door, in millions of small apartments and families' transformed basements all over much of the world, people like Sarah faced the same empty spaces on their own quiet evenings.

But the mind looks for ways out even when people don't see them. At lunch one day, Sarah suddenly said that the concerns that had so vexed her for many months were now fading—much to her surprise. They were just fading away. The strange thing, she said, was that now she really cared less about where she lived, or why. But it didn't feel like giving up. It didn't feel like surrender or succumbing to powerlessness. It seemed that all of that was becoming irrelevant.

She was discovering, rather than exactly learning, something new, it seemed. The whole thing of living well, being respected and so on—the classic Sarah—seemed somehow behind her, no longer in front of her.

She didn't know it at first, but despite everything, or maybe because of it, Sarah was getting old in the ancient way. She was getting ready to contribute what old people can impart to the world they will soon have to leave to its own devices. Changing the world and banishing prejudice was part of the person she once was, not the person she was becoming—someone who understood being old and where the knowledge of the old lay. She was beginning to see that she would never contribute any more in the old way she had, but she didn't see yet what that would mean in the way of her contributing something deeper to the world than even what she had given before.

# Chapter Six:

# Going Deep-Questions and Answers

*...And the point is to live everything. Live the questions now. Perhaps then, someday far in the future, you will gradually, without even noticing it, live your way into the answer.*

**Rainer Maria Rilke,**
**Letters to a Young Poet**


*...So I asked God for the umpteenth time...*
*"What can I do with the rest of my life that will have real meaning? That will help young people to see old age as something to look forward to? ...*
*Finally, an answer came that I think will get me out of bed in the morning. A true sacred vision:*
*to develop a listening heart...*

**Sarah Z.**


Most inward explorations are unintentional in the beginning, and they are never linear. They most often come when the successes, pleasures, and security offered by everyday life disappear, perhaps suddenly. They come when what one would like to change in the world seems unlikely to bend. The experience of some great, nearly intolerable joy may also lead to inwardness, or to a mystical and inexplicable experience. The need to make a deeper exploration of life and one's beliefs can come when one feels weak, and sometimes when one gets close to death. This is not to say that death and depth go hand in hand; they may, or they may not. Some people reject their lifelong beliefs at death or shortly before; others who were never "spiritual" find some version of a world beyond the material comforting and meaningful about the same time.

Still others find that exploring what we might call "ultimate," "deep," or "impenetrable" realities—however they come—may give them a growing degree of freedom and comfort. They may begin with memories of failures or unfulfilled expectations, and then may trail into forgotten dreams and heartfelt emotions long ago buried for the sake of survival. These different memories and experiences often are not easy to manage when they surface into consciousness. But if they can be allowed to flow in even just a little, they can change people or remind them of who they used to be—and maybe even who they really are. This creates a relief few of us get the chance to know in daily life.

"Going deep" is about asking and answering questions about yourself and your life and getting answers to questions you may not have asked. If you go deep enough, past the anxiety and feelings of guilt or anger and even—with preparation—past terrible memories, you might well find a place of deep relaxation, and breathe a long, tension-releasing sigh. The questions that seemed so important may prove not to be, and the ones you never asked may have already been answered.

## What Did I Give Up?

Going deep usually starts with going back, looking at who we are and what might have been. Sarah began to ask herself, "What if?" What if she had not wasted time being who she wasn't? She had asked herself these questions off and on for years, but now she had time to follow them through.

Sarah first asked if she had lived too much in her mother's and other people's shadows. Had she pushed her real self down, just to be the powerful person she became? What had that been worth, if now at the end she was not very powerful at all? Could she have done something different?

> I don't know what I would have really been if I had really done it my way. I mean, I had a long list of things I had to do, like get married, have children, be smart enough to hold down a job the whole time, figure out how to make all that happen without getting upset or down when things didn't go my way. It was a very difficult list, I thought.

> I think it would have been better if it were my own list, because I could have found out what my answers to my questions would be. So, for example, when I was in the sixth grade, I was overweight and my mother thought that was not a good thing to be. She was forever putting me on diets and getting me black skirts and all of that. Now, I managed pretty well with her idea of what I should be like, but I never found out what I would

*have really been like and whether or not anybody would
have liked me that way...*

*After my divorce and all that, my daughter said to me;
"I see you have another person you're spending time
with." Then she said, "Is it another guy who'll look good
in the pictures or is it really somebody you have fun
with?" And I thought, how does she know all that?
But she did. I learned a lot from that. Because I did
have to have someone to look good in the pictures;
that was the given. The pictures were more real to me
than my own life. That kind of thing doesn't make any
sense to me at all now. I think I have since learned how
not to do the pictures so much, but I could have used a
lot more time on that—a lot more. So, let's say I spent
80% of my time on the pictures and 20% in real life.
I could have reversed that.*

*So now I wonder, related to that, what I think of myself.
I want to be thinking of how I treated other people.
It's not about my ever hitting anyone, screaming at
them, calling them names. I know I have not a lot to
repent for in that way. But it has to do with my
intention. That's hard.*

Sarah looked at these questions for many months and
found some important answers. Yes, her worries about looks,
others' opinions, her mother's judgement, and so on had
taken her off track, even for years. While she believed she
had never actually caused great pain, certain intentions had
been part of a darker side of who she was, and to sit with
these was not easy.

But that was who she had been, and the errors in it were clear now, or would never be. Some of it mattered, and some of it did not. Yes, she was still a proud person, and conscious of how she appeared to others. She was no saint and would die that way. But so it was.

## What About God? And Me?

The more limited we become, the more our own answers are unsatisfactory, the more likely it is that we will ask where some other guidance might be, or was, and what is expected of us. The growing limitations caused by her illness and the death that now seemed to be coming soon brought back three questions: "Who am I?" "What is God—if he exists?" "What does God want from or for me?"

Sarah had always wanted to contribute, to do good for others. It was her reason for being. All that she did to be herself she did to be *useful*—a force for change, a powerhouse not for herself but for the benefit of others. Whether God had set her on this path or not she didn't know, and for a long time, she didn't care. Her insight and wisdom had made her powerful, and she had used her power not to manufacture boxes or invest more money for herself, but to make a difference.

Now, as her body and life in general began to slip from her grasp, she could not really live the life of purpose she had long felt was at her core—certainly not in the way she had. So, was there a God and did he see what was happening here? What did he want from her if he was there at all? Why this loss of her best quality and her most important work? What was she supposed to do now?

*It's the lack of purpose. That's what changes as I get worse. There's not a lot I can do now without losing my breath, without being very tired afterwards. In the early days of the Parkinson's, let's say years one to ten, I was still doing everything I did before. I was working. I was studying. I was dating. It was great. And all I had to do was take this one pill and it would keep at bay all the symptoms. Wow. Now my symptoms are so great I can't do that. And so I can't do the things I love to do. And mostly I can't do the things that give me purpose.*
*So, what's the point? I don't get that. What's the point? Some people would say the point is to be alive and to be outside in the sun, but I never was that kind of person. So I don't see how I'm going to be that now.*

*I've never been the kind of person who thinks life is just there and you just live in it. I wish I had at some point seen that, loved that, but I never did. I love a sunset, it's great. Water is great—the ocean. Great. But I don't connect that to purpose. You know, God's taking care of all that; he doesn't need me to take care of the sunsets and the ocean. I think he must have had some reason for creating me, but I don't know what it is.*

Many give the job of finding purpose to the God of their belief. Sarah had expected her God would give her some of the smaller stuff to do while he did sunsets and planets and so on, but it seemed the answer had not come, and her options were now disappearing. So, what had her job been?

Had she failed him? Had he failed her? Where was he now? What was she doing now? The question bounced about in her head and heart and came back many times. She asked God these and other questions, but for a long time she thought she heard, saw, or felt no answers.

## Answers to Questions Not Asked

Sarah had been unhappy for a while, both in general and with specific people and circumstances. She grieved not being who she had been and still wanted to be. She was tired and lost. She often was angry with the person she was closest to in the world—her best friend ever since they had been children. Her friend never seemed to "get" Sarah's anger, she thought, which made Sarah even angrier. Her friend had plenty to do and a busy, happy life, but she took time every day, sometimes two or three times, to check on Sarah. She would ask how she was, have a chat, and express her love. Sarah both loved and hated the contact. She needed it, perhaps, and wished she didn't. Why wasn't she stronger than that?

Things inside her began to shift, though she couldn't say why, or even exactly how. It almost seemed that since she had lost a good deal of power, she was finding she didn't need it anyway. She didn't need to have her friend's calls be along the lines of a Sarah-approved script. What had made her feel frustrated and angry about the calls just...didn't anymore. A small change in attitude, but very big. To not be angry even though nothing had changed? What her friend said was fine; why did she need her to be different?

She could listen or not; she didn't need anyone or anything to change. She had to think about this:

*I had to put my tush in the chair, which frankly is very uncomfortable. It is...really, it's not great to sit in! And I sat there anyway, and I thought, well, that's pretty interesting. I don't know if I love this feeling, but I don't hate it, like I did the others. I didn't like being angry all the time. I didn't even like being angry at my best friend from my childhood.*

*She's a great person to be angry at. She simply refuses to take it in. She says, "Oh alright, I'll call you back tomorrow." I wasn't...I couldn't even come up with anything to be angry with her about. In the past, I would have been really angry because I didn't want to hear about how things were for her when they weren't so good for me. But now I think, so, I guess that's my choice. Listen, hang up, or say, "Thanks for sharing. I gotta go."*

Sarah saw this as a significant change in herself, and toward peace rather than greater agitation. What a relief. It is the little things that actually mark the biggest shifts in the internal structures of a mind, and its way of seeing the world and defining a self.

### More Relief

She also had a few experiences with her most difficult human contacts at the time: the staff who cared for her. Her new reactions—seemingly coming out of nowhere—surprised her. She usually felt angry with people whom she felt had treated her rudely and inappropriately. She had been angry about her powerlessness and the resistance to her attempts to contribute. But now sometimes she didn't. She felt pangs of compassion for the people who seemed disgusted or harassed by her, and she sometimes not only saw, but felt, their side of things as if it were her own. Poorly paid. Overworked. Here she sat, a privileged woman, telling them what to do.

She saw her own struggle also with a strangely new compassion for herself, rather than resistance or hurt. She saw both herself and her caregiver of the moment, struggling in a system that had put them both in difficult roles. She was not sure what to do about these new reactions:

> So, it's been happening. I've been traveling through this very strange terrain, and I thought, well, I don't know if we have a book anymore [because it was to be about how bad things are for the aging, as you might recall], but this is really where I am. I'm in maybe a better space. I don't know. But I wonder if that's possible. If you can get through the hatred and anger and all of that, then it looks like it's possible.

## Pendulum Swings

Of course, the process was not all in one direction, as it never is. When small mental changes happen, one doesn't become a new person altogether—now happy—and peaceful. Certainly not Sarah, who resisted most changes more easily than she accepted them. The old hopes and habits of mind were dying hard.

Sarah continued to vacillate between staying where she was and moving somewhere that might be better. When the next brochure on a new senior living opportunity came in, she would rush out to see the place, sure this one would be it. A spark of genius one day would have her calling her friends to consider converting a motel into a shared living facility with dining and staff in the office. Not a bad idea. But looking at a run-down motel off the highway one Sunday in the rain, Sarah had to watch that dream too, wash down the drain.

She kept changing her room around for maximum space, ordered new curtains, and bought new office paper trays, cabinets, and wall shelves. It never fully worked. She was frustrated by another ridiculous wait for help on something stupid like replacing the old blinds.

Hardest of all, she was increasingly depressed and disappointed, even angry, because the end of the week was always coming, dragging with it those long hours of emptiness. These did not go away, and their sadness continued to oppress her. The quiet of the halls was complete. Everyone had a life but she and the others around her, left in their rooms like worn out dolls. Even though her family came for visits, the visits were not long enough. Sarah's most terrible enemies continued to stalk the silent halls those long days and nights: loneliness, time, nothingness.

Still, into this set of objections and unmet hopes came some surprises for her and for the rest of us: times when she wasn't angry, impatient, or hurt by our absences, and even times when she felt glad about something intangible.

It began to be okay. The whole thing began to be okay. It not only was what it was, but she was finding herself ready to let that be. It just wasn't her anymore. The pendulum swings became less extreme. She finally turned down a new facility she had really thought might be different:

> *I really thought I might've been in that new place,*
> *you know? But then I decided not to go. Wow.*
> *That's interesting. I don't hate it here. It's ugly.*
> *I wouldn't make it like this, but so...Maybe I say that*
> *nurse is terrible. She won't help me. So, I won't ask her.*
> *I'll ask someone else. Who else is around? That's really a*
> *different use of energy than I've had in the past.*
> *And it's not so bad, you know, it's really not.*
> *And it's lasting...I'm still there.*

Sometimes now, the backswing of the pendulum did not send her so far into anger and bleakness.

Again, many people would not think of these changes as particularly deep or earth-shaking, but finding some things simply fading as desperate concerns can have a strangely expanding feeling and significant effects. For Sarah, changes in her level of relaxation and enjoyment seemed to come right out of her surrender to what was rather than fighting it.

That seemed like a big lesson from somewhere. Those changes meant that she was less interested in making the next move she had so sought; she almost saw that she was becoming unable to make the move anyway. The ripple was tremendous; she hassled her family and the staff less, and some days she seemed calm and even content. New ways of living began to present themselves in the spaces she had until then used for being upset and lost. One of them was to give her great joy, and a way home.

### Rediscovering a New Way of Believing

A few years before, Sarah had asked God the specific question of what she could do for others as she aged. I don't know that she believed God had given her the answer, but one came. She remembered something she had said to herself about the future she had then just begun. Now it seemed more relevant and less abstract than it had been. You will remember Sarah's words at the start of this book:

> *Finally, an answer came that I think will get me out of bed in the morning. A true sacred vision: to develop a listening heart...My question for God was not prescriptive, but descriptive...Perhaps instead of monitoring all the things I can no longer DO in the world, I can expand and develop what I can BE in the world—for myself, my children, my grandchildren, and others who may benefit from the presence of a listening heart. Fortunately, I don't think it is something that I will age out of.*

That was good, and important, and she surely felt more inspired to listen these days. But now that also wasn't going to be enough. It was important, but it wasn't God, or something beyond herself that would let her look farther than her own horizon.

She had written that a while ago, and she wasn't sure she had done a very good job of listening in the meantime. She was trying to be better about it, and it was getting much easier. But she was living that old future now, and the death that would end it was close. The stakes were higher, and a listening heart began to mean listening for more than the sake of others. It meant listening for other voices, for herself.

Sarah began, without much fanfare or discussion, to explore a God that was not the soft-focus one she had tried to imagine or explored with her friends in an earlier, softer time. They could talk about nature and sunsets and even meditation, but it hadn't worked for her then and she certainly needed more now. She needed life and people and strength because these were what she was losing.

Perhaps Sarah had an increasing sense of peace, but she was still scared, and had not lost the desire to be useful or live in the midst of people. After all, she was beginning to see them differently, and to crave their company in new ways. She needed to find what she had missed, why she had been unhappy, and where the subtle changes in her acceptance and even greater satisfaction might lead.

It was a typical Sarah process: active, purposeful, full of people and light and rebellion. No soft focus, and no sunsets. But where she would go proved to be as deep as she had ever gone or could go in the time she had.

Sometimes, simply not having the old options any more can loosen the concrete of an ego, and some fresh water may bubble up through the cracks like the first seeps from an underground stream. In that underground stream may be some fresh water that had been buried deep, some inkling of who one was before, in one's innocence, in the few wide and open times before one had had to grow up a bit. Sometimes the spiritual place one knew as a child—church on Sunday, temple on Saturday, the mosque, the prayer grove—a prayer or a psalm someone always said—will come up, not with a message so much as a memory that seems to have a mysterious gravitational pull. It may be of an idea, or a place, or a set of beliefs, or something else. Most of all, it is a longing. Sarah remembered holding her father's hand in the synagogue of her childhood.

Sarah's father had been a devout Jew and had brought her to that faith—or more importantly for her, to the synagogue, for many years. It was a place of some unfathomable power for her; it was also where she most felt her father's love not only for her, but for something called God which she could feel, maybe, but not understand. She needed that sense of something bigger now, like that which she had felt standing by his side in all those services of her childhood.

Feeling peaceful, as she had been, was good, and feeling it grow was rather enriching. But when she had been very young, there had been a God. She felt the need of a presence like that now, or at least she wanted to test whether something like that might be real. Her own original faith, about which she knew something, and for which she had some feeling—albeit as we shall see, not all of it good—

seemed to call her back. Something or someone seemed to be reminding her of who she was, and what was most important for her about being human. The wisdom was not to be given by her to others but received from them.

She had tried nearly everything else before she dared to darken the door of Judaism again; she would try that now. Without really knowing why, Sarah found herself drawn to a place and faith she had not valued for most of her adult life. Her father had gotten her there when she was small, but now her grown self took the next steps forward.

That Sarah was Jewish in heritage and Judaism was the faith she had learned as a small child now seemed to matter in ways it hadn't. For most of her life she had thought; "So what?" How could it matter to a modern woman raising two daughters and running a successful business what religion or ethnic heritage she was? Even if something metaphysical or spiritual were out there, did it matter if it were Jewish or something else?

But Judaism was her tie to her father. He had taught Sarah about his own faith deeply held and deeply felt. She loved him and he loved her: this mattered most of all. She was happy to be with him in that place which meant so much to him in ways she couldn't fully understand. When she left her faith and abjured the temples, it was because of him also.

When she was still very young, she was undone by what she saw as her father's blindness to the terrible and unfair burden of his beliefs. One day after learning to read, she read the prayers of Yom Kippur as everyone chanted them. She couldn't believe what they said: that her father was a sinner and a bad person. Her father, the kindest, most gentle person she had ever known! She told him this was crazy and unfair and made no sense at all. He told her to ignore the words, but she could not. She would have liked a faith of joy and light, but:

> What I got was Rosh Hashana and Yom Kippur:
> "What have you done wrong? See here, what can we get
> you to fix? You must apologize. You must've..."
> Oy, it was a big drag. And I didn't see how it helped me
> anyway.

She began to pull away from Judaism though her father told her the words were not important for her to know—it was the feeling. Perhaps it became youthful rebellion as well, or the subtle influence of her domineering and non-observant mother. Whatever the reason, after a time she left it far behind.

Still, over all the years of her lack of interest in her root faith and ethnicity, she had not lost a belief that there might be a God. We have seen how it expressed itself in exasperation that he seemed to have no interest in anything that might guide her.

Sarah was shocked when her father announced on his deathbed that he no longer believed in God. She couldn't help but wonder what must have happened to turn her father, a good man and a believer, into an angry, disbelieving man just then; she told him it was not good timing.

She wondered now because she needed his faith or at least wanted to understand what it had meant to him. Maybe she hoped it would lead her home to some place she could not fully imagine, back to when he believed, and she believed in him. Something there about love and a power beyond understanding must have surfaced. She decided to go home, but first only for a visit.

## The Return

The Jewish connection perhaps pulled her; or perhaps the God in whom she had a frayed faith loosened her heart again. One day, she met a delightful woman who suggested she come to a service. "You'll love it," the woman said.
She was vibrant and happy, and she was genuine.
With no fanfare or even comment, Sarah went back one day to the place to which the woman had invited her.
The place wasn't exactly a synagogue—she was glad about that. It was a Hillel House, a place of gathering for Jewish youth and others who support social justice causes.
People were dancing and singing.

So, with the help of a strong and clearly believing younger woman, she walked back into her deepest past, to the God of her father. Her reaction surprised her, and it quickly grew in power. Referring to something I had said when we had first started to work together she said:

> So, a long time ago, you said you thought that people
> who were aware that they have a terminal disease
> started to go back to the roots of their religion, right?

I thought, Ah!!! You won't catch me in any temples just 'cause I'm dyin'!

Well, I did catch myself in one and it was at Hillel, not at the regular temple, and it was being led by a woman who is probably a little younger than I am. Quite a bit maybe, I don't know; but she was full of joy. Beautiful voice—it was her gift. And she was singing away and doing all kinds of music and I thought, "Oh my God, this is a fun place!" If my dad had been involved that way...this, I really liked. So, I thought, uh oh, maybe I will be returning to my roots because I'd really like to come here. You know, this is cool.

So afterwards the group had lunch and several subsequent meetings. They invited the caregiver who drove me there to have lunch with them and there was a cheek pincher in the group. I had to rename him the Cheek Cruncher...because he grabbed ahold of my cheek. No one had done this to me since I was fourteen and my grandmother was at the other end of it. My grandmother had done that my whole life—pinching of the cheeks. You know, you don't come up to somebody and just pinch their cheeks. So, I was like "S'cuse me, sir..." He said, "I love these cheeks. Look at these cheeks!" I said, "Good, all right. I can gain 10 more pounds and you'll really love my cheeks!" He said, "Oh, I love that cheek." I said, "Listen, it's still mine as far as I know".... But I think...he's just a sweet, old man. And it was just a very welcoming, nice group. I liked it.

The matter must have reminded her of her father's faith more than her anger and his final stance. Her enthusiasm even trumped the pinching. The leader came over and broke up the scene and began to speak to Sarah, welcoming her.

*I really liked her and I said, "You know, I'd really like to come back and I would like to be able to participate more, so where could I go to learn the service that you're doing?" She said, "You just want to learn the Hebrew of this service, or do you want to learn to speak Hebrew?" I said, "No, I just wanted to learn the service." She said, "Oh, well that would be fun. I'll teach you."*
*I said, "Really?" She said, "Yeah, sure."*

*So that was very appealing to me. I thought, wow, this would be very nice...We talked about why I wanted to learn Hebrew, which is so that I can say a prayer for my dad. Because when he died, I did not know enough Hebrew to read the Hebrew prayer for the dead and I really wanted to. So, with my motivation in mind, she arrived Sunday at seven and I now know half of the prayer.*

*I find that so much more pleasurable than I ever did, and I don't know why, but it calls me like, you know... "Hey you! You've been over there with those people. Those aren't your people!" Which I find fascinating.*

*So how do you do that...Split yourself all up? The one who hates what it was and the one who loves what it is...Dunno, but I guess life is like that. You have to take*

*some stuff that you hate along with the other stuff*
*that's very yummy.*

*And also, for me, anyway, the cells in my body*
*reverberate to Hebrew in a way that they don't*
*reverberate to something else. So, I get into this room the*
*other day and they're all playing instruments and they're*
*singing! And I thought oh yeah, I'll go over there. That's*
*me. That's where I belong. You know, I don't know the*
*words, I don't know the music. I don't care. I like it.*

Sarah began to feel more and more at home in the faith
she had run from in anger when she was a child. The music,
the words, even the prayers began to feel like home, which
was a kind of spiritual experience in itself. To feel "at home,"
not as she had known it with a domineering mother for
whom she could do nothing right, but as the phrase is meant
to suggest: peaceful, secure, making a person ready to take
on what is coming with a sense that she is not alone. True
home means that what is hard or frightening isn't all there
is, that something bigger and full of acceptance is still there,
and always will be there. True home may mean the place of
your people, a cultural home as well as a personal one.
Her experience of Judaism began to feel like that. Here were
new words for her vocabulary: home, faith community,
Jewish roots, one's own people.

To Sarah, from New York City like many in the group at
Hillel, the experience was both meaningful and fun, and
such a surprise as to be a new lease on her shortening life.
It was home in lots of ways. It gave her something to think

about that wasn't negative and yet didn't require her to invest in false hopes. She studied more Hebrew songs and chants. She learned and sang them with great feeling. She visited with the rabbi. She read. She learned the prayer for the dead that she wanted to say for her father. She learned it in Hebrew. She wanted to study the history of her people. She understood, she *understood*, a little bit about faith and its purpose. She felt it all in her body. In her head the old melodies danced, and the words spoke to her:

> *I had my Hebrew lesson. I swear I'm enjoying the Hebrew. That's so funny to me 'cause I so hated that when I was young...You know, as I come round the bend on the words I know what the next sound is gonna be, I'm like, "Oh, I know that now." And it's really fun for me. Plus, I like my teacher; she's very upbeat without being wushy-gushy. And she's been very positive about my progress, which I always like too. So that's all good. A very good thing, actually.*

Sarah talked about something else happening to her that reflected that childhood level of connection with the divine or the larger than life. She felt a little off in her prayers; she was missing something. She didn't have it yet, and she knew why:

> *Not yet, because the pace of it isn't right and I don't know how I know that. That's the piece that interests me...I think I know it's not right 'cause I stood next to my father all those years and listened to him say it. So, it doesn't sound like...that the emphasis is in the*

*right place. But I'm getting the letters and I'm getting the*
*words and slowly I'm managing.*

The company and the lessons all fit her desires in another
way as well; she was less lonely. Sarah wanted to be busy, and
to be accepted and valued at the same time was a great bonus.
She was all of these within her newly adopted Jewish community:

*And my schedule is so much fuller now than it was*
*maybe even when we started this. I feel a little bit more,*
*uh, comfortable there.*

Okay, so it wasn't all perfect; it didn't all fit or feel perfect.
But as her father had said when she was little, don't worry so
much about that. She loved to think of metaphors for it.
All the other things she'd tried, maybe they had been food of
a kind. But this one was different—in a different bowl,
and it filled her up:

*Completely different bowl. And you don't maybe like the*
*color of it so much, but hey, you get that bowl and you*
*feel like, man, this is oatmeal. You know, it's so*
*comfortable. It's warm.*

Sarah said she was becoming Jewish again:

*My kids are gonna be very amused at that because for a*
*long time we didn't have any Judaism in my house.*
*I don't know why really, but we just didn't have it.*

Her children had been practicing their faith for years now,
but Sarah had not, until now. She said she was

*...going back to my religion of origin. Nice to have my*
*own little piece of history back.*

Studying Judaism and practicing it in the way she was, Sarah found solace and comfort in coming home. But she found more:

*So, it all feels right in a number of ways. Yes, there is*
*something about it that's a shared life. But there are*
*other pieces that I've been reading now that speak to*
*this notion of wholeness that I'm moving towards–*
*being part of a whole.*

*And that whole is not only Judaism, of course, it's the*
*whole plan, the whole everything. The whole*
*humanness, the whole. I don't think bigger than that.*
*And for that, I might need Judaism. I have no idea why*
*or how, but I just want to be with it in a different way.*

## Act of Faith

Sarah was indeed very much of this world. For her, this life was what she had, and though it was slipping away, she would live every last minute of it. Her act of faith was to go back to who she had been, hoping the person there would be herself.

Now it seemed Sarah did not feel drawn to the other kinds of spiritual or mystical experience that she had sought in other faiths. She had less desire to engage in the New Age practices of visioning or past-life regression, nor the popular versions of meditation. She was not a mystic. She spoke of no overwhelming conversion experience, and she did not reach enlightenment—unless she did at the time of her death. The spiritual, or her deepest self, to her was in this world, perhaps best defined by the words love and belonging, the core and the expansion of her "listening heart."

Sarah's deepest hope as the end neared was that she would die knowing she had been kind, and while she was still the Sarah she and others knew and loved. The wholeness and sense of homecoming that her faith was giving her let her find some ways to do that. It offered open arms large enough to hold her fear and offered her love she had thought she would never have. For her, her homecoming came mostly from fellowship with others who felt deeply familiar, the liturgy that reverberated in her, and that sense of belonging at the root of it all. Striking out from home, she could do anything. That would likely be enough, and more and more, it was looking like it might be all she had time for.

## Getting Closer to Goodbye

As she began to feel herself growing into patience, peace, belonging, and even wholeness, other concerns began to drop away. She slowly began to find the courage to begin to say her goodbyes to herself as well as others, and the peace of mind not to be overwhelmingly afraid of death in its growingly concrete form. Afraid of pain, yes, but who isn't? Death, well...it was what it was, and it wasn't going to be different if she worried about it. Now, for the first time, in a practical way, Sarah began to believe she could end her life when it was time.

But the faith she was taking on again and all her new awareness and comfort were soon to be put to the ultimate test. Sarah was going fast, and her world was changing quickly.

**Strong Enough?**

More and more, Sarah lived in three parallel realities: the one of her body and brain; the one of her Parkinsonian delusions; and the one of people, memories, questions and a new/old world of faith that all seemed to hold some interesting mysteries of peace. Could the latter hold their own against the former?

Though her body changes were frightening, Sarah was more afraid of her delusions. The latter meant the loss of her mind, her most precious asset and the core of her being. The confusion of worlds came often now:

> *[I was] in my room, but it was not really my room, but it was my room back and forth, back and forth. But then there was the wedding that I was still anticipating being somewhere for. It has been very persistent, this wedding. And the way that I knew it was my room was that I had anchors, you know? Oh yes, that's a picture I know and that's fine.*
>
> *Day after day. So, on it goes, and each day I would say [to the staff], "So what time is the wedding?" And each day they would say—the helpers—"There's no wedding, Sarah, you're not going anywhere. You're in assisted living." And I think, "Ha! No I'm not." But I never*

*said anything about that. Went back into my room,*
*anchored myself... ah, well, I guess I could be here,*
*because there are all these stupid things in my room that*
*I can anchor on.*

The Parkinson's was becoming all the frightening things the doctors had said it would be. Could she do this part? She was used to Parkinson's being a lonely business in this world—people thought they understood it, but how could they? Now, even she could hardly believe or understand it. She was angry and afraid, and as the world of her delusions intruded on the world she knew, she became ever more alone:

*This last go round was really uncomfortable because it*
*seemed like everybody had left at the end of the day.*
*They left me where I was, wherever that was. So I was*
*in some... I was in the exact same structure as I have*
*here, but it was not here...it was a last railroad train*
*car... And each one was the same as the one before it,*
*but it wasn't in the right place. Instead of being here,*
*I was wherever the wedding was. Yes. There was nobody*
*left from the wedding to take me back home. So I was*
*just like stranded on this train somewhere....*

*So anyhow, I got frightened and I went to the door*
*[of her place] to see if it went where I thought it went.*
*Like, things going by outside would make it the railroad*
*car, or is there a walkway like there is here? And sure*
*enough there it was, the old walkway. So I said, ah,*
*I see. Okay, so it's true. I am here, but where are the*

*nurses? They should be here, they're not here. So I*
*pushed my button and nobody came for a few minutes,*
*but then all of a sudden out came two people, both of*
*whom I know to be nurses on this floor. And they said,*
*"What's wrong?" And I said, "Nothing. I just didn't see*
*anybody for a long time and I didn't know where you*
*were." She said, "Oh, we're in a meeting. It's all fine.*
*Go back to sleep." So I did.*

Perhaps the most frightening of these experiences happened one night when Sarah thought the building was on fire. In the midst of a Parkinsonian delusion, she pulled the alarm in her room, went down the hall to wake up the residents, got her coat, and went outside—to total calm. There was no fire. She was afraid now. What was going on? Didn't people see what was going on? She was found outside and taken back in. How did she feel afterwards? Not only afraid, but deeply afraid, and lost in the space between two worlds that had begun to overlap. Even more of a problem with this was her fear: she was afraid she would be declared mentally incompetent, despite the fact that the delusions would pass and she would take back her reality. What could help her with this? The gathering clouds in her mind threatened the tiny bit of freedom she had left. Faith seemed a paltry defense against the loss of her mind and perhaps her last bit of dignity:

*I'd like to say how painful this is for me not to have*
*choice in my life. How really amazing it is to find that*
*I can be awakened at some unknown hour in the early*

*morning with a huge noise that is supposed to be a fire*
*alarm but coming out of my delusions, but which I'm*
*not even sure are dreams. Sometimes they feel so real*
*that I am totally at the mercy of other people who come*
*to tell me whether or not I am awake or asleep, psychotic*
*or not. That's what I'd like to say, but I'm afraid that*
*they would lock me up. And that's not a flight of fancy.*
*I must be careful these days about what I say and do for*
*fear that others will become so afraid of me that my*
*choices will become even more restricted than they are*
*right now.*

Thankfully, she could indeed confront all this disastrous change with her discoveries from going deep and her new-old life of faith. All those discoveries were molding into the shape of Sarah's own self, or she was becoming more of herself as they grew in her.

## Yes

She was finding her own personal faith in what she felt truly mattered: accepting others and maybe even herself. She was finding home in all the senses of that word, and a sense of something bigger that she could count on— even if she had no idea why or how. She found that peace was a lovely, subtle feeling that crept into difficult situations and eased them. It had to do partly with surrender, but also with memory and community.

Her own expanded version of the world was proving truly important and lasting, even when put to serious tests.

Her inner quiet and outer connections did not quash her fears or ease her suffering, but they paralleled them with strength and a growing wisdom that went beyond them. In this world, even if she was afraid and in various kinds of pain, she could give and be given to. She had ground to stand on. It gave her something she could give to others; not in words always, but in her actions and the feelings she evoked in others. She might not reach some grand goal or even God, but she had gotten close enough, which was good enough.

# Chapter Seven:
# The Last, Best Lessons–
# Caring and Connecting

*We give because someone gave to us.*
*We give because nobody gave to us.*

*We give because giving has changed us.*
*We give because giving could have changed us.*

*We have been better for it,*
*We have been wounded by it–*

*...Giving is, first and every time, hand to hand,*
*Mine to yours, yours to mine.*

*You gave me blue and I gave you yellow.*
*Together we are simple green. You gave me*

*What you did not have, and I gave you*
*What I had to give–together, we made*

*Something greater from the difference.*

**Alberto Ríos**
*From "When Giving is All We Have"*

No matter how much the many changes coming now preoccupied her, and no matter the peace and clarity she felt coming also, Sarah sensed that something else about her life was yet to be resolved. This was the most important part of the Sarah she had lost some time ago; perhaps her experiences with her faith contributed to her growing desire to find it.

She felt her mother had determined early on that loving and accepting her was unnecessary and undeserved. When she determined to show her mother who she was and prove her worth, Sarah tried to overcome this judgment of her mother's, too. She must be lovable and acceptable, mustn't she? It seemed others were.

But Sarah's efforts to make love happen were complicated and could be problematic. Her emotional demands on the one hand, and her need for independence and control on the other, tended to push partners away. Or *she* pushed them away. But friends—she made and kept the ones she made. She exhausted, maddened, and charmed them, and when she could, she listened to them. Maybe there was something important in that.

Not that she hadn't looked for intimacy and unconditional love, romance, a soul mate; she had looked for them everywhere. She had offered much and demanded it, too. Yet somehow, she never could see what was offered: how much people loved her—not only liked her, but truly loved, even were *in love* with her. What she wanted had never, ever proved to be exactly what she got—the nearly universal experience—but she would not settle for less. Her own role in her loneliness had never been very clear to her.

Now, as one can imagine, she was grieved about facing this difficult time with no significant other, no partner, to call her own. She felt empty in that way, and it was late now to fill the void. She saw togetherness everywhere: in her friends' partners, husbands and wives and in her family;

even her dear private helpers went home at the end of the day to tend to their own lives. Or so it seemed. With a flock of some fifty chickens to attend by nightfall, I perhaps had the least painful and most irritating reason for leaving her company. Who could be jealous of a flock of chickens?

Now, with the situation as it was and the changes that were coming, the whole matter of love and acceptance shifted a bit. Some intimate relationships were no longer really feasible, but somehow others were also rewarding, and perhaps more necessary now. Strange. A prince in shining armor might be wonderful, but other kinds of connections were increasingly important. She had always felt romance was a conditional kind of love, and now she needed something other than that. In her contradictory search for love and independence, the large nut of personal grief— practically the size of a coconut and just as hard—was about to crack.

Sarah loved deeply and intensely, she thought, but perhaps she desired deeply and resisted intensely also. Failure would hurt too much, and so sometimes anger and coldness replaced the old feelings of guilt and grief for again not being good enough.

She had asked questions about her way of caring for a while now: Why had she thought the biggest goal to achieve in her life was to be stronger and better than her mother ever thought she could be? If she had just been herself... but who was that?

From the outside, it seemed Sarah wanted to love, but

looked for ways to see why people *didn't* love her, or why she should not love them. Why, she asked herself, did she pick people who just weren't quite good enough, or mean, or unavailable? Could one accept that, even with all their foibles and shortcomings, some people really did love her, and maybe were just who they were? Sarah was more complicated than any popular psychology ideas people attempted to apply to her. She was like the rest of us really are: full of contradictions, dreams never reached, impossible desires, and a tendency to confuse one emotion, like hurt, for another, like anger. In later life, her focus on what she lacked had been preventing her from seeing what else was there to have and to hold.

But what then was there, for a woman who so wanted to love and belong, when the world began to slip away, and she was actually and truly alone on a journey we all must take by ourselves? Who at least was nearby? She wanted freedom, and she was lonely—which can be a natural consequence of freedom. She wanted love, but not if it made it hard for her to remember who she was. The middle ground was slippery; sometimes it seemed that she and everyone she loved were fighting in the mud.

**Lessons**

All her best lessons had come slowly, and sometimes the understanding came even later. The answers may have been in the back of the textbook, but they made no sense if she couldn't figure out the problem on her own first.

In her losing fights and failed resistance to her necessary

surrenders, she discovered realities larger than she was, from community to faith and heritage, and even to her own nature. But something else also began to mature: a fuller picture of who she was and what she wanted to give.

She had began to see how the people in her life really were wonderful, or at least fine just as they were, or at the very least, not going to change into the beings of her dreams. It was a matter of coming to see what she truly wanted from herself and from them, even from the world—not what she thought her mother wanted her to want, or what she felt she lacked. Crack. An egg falls off the wall; Sarah would not be put together again in the same way.

It just took a bit of time and more loss for her last, best discovery to break through. It had to do with finding some new room for others and herself as the old, hard struggles for success and worthiness fell away.

**More Questions**

Sarah had been asking deeper questions than before, or more intimate ones. Not why she was treated like a child by a controlling staff, but why that mattered to her at all; not what her illness actually had cost her, but what it had forced her to give up. How valuable was what she had lost going to be in the next few months she had left?

She could not be the woman who made things different anymore. So, what was the point of trying? That driving sense of purpose was still there, and there was the work on this book that gave her a possible legacy of something meaningful. But the book would also have to chronicle this sense of not being able to make a difference anymore, the end of living for a purpose that had come with her failing body. Or was that entirely true? She wanted to contribute something to her new community of faith. But what did they need that she could offer?

It is hard in the midst of an apparently important life to discover that the answers to your most poignant questions are often right in front of you. You reject them because they seem silly or unimportant. But it may be that the lessons are never as simple-minded and irrelevant as they always sound.

Sarah's great discovery was nothing she would have expected, nor even thought, was all that worthy of her. Then one day it slipped out: what she truly loved and made her joyful was nothing grand at all; in fact, she had done it for years. She just hadn't realized how much she loved it, and that it lay at the very heart of her dear, vulnerable, essential being. It came to her in a conversation with me, as she was thinking about yet another new place to live, the last one she considered.

Sarah sat for a minute. She got quiet. She looked around her room, increasingly full of growing collections of papers, projects, furniture, cabinets, new wire storage racks in the now bursting closets, additional special shelves, two desks, and still the paintings and the sofa and the sink and the fronds. Why had she not seen that about herself? This trying to fix things up to look good—that wasn't all that important. What she really loved to do: create her own special art and put people together out of excitement and joy, those were.

Why not? If neither was grand nor promised to save the world, what of that?

*The new place I'm looking at is beautiful and I like things that are beautiful. Why live in a place that's ugly? And why have people crammed in, like we are here?*

*We should have more space... maybe I want to type up ninety-seven things while my assistant is doing something else. We can't do that here. And when I've worked in the past with others, I've had that kind of space. Maybe I would even make a necklace simultaneously. Wow. That would be good.*

*Doing different things...all kinds of things...I would love that. That would be pure joy for me.... Oh, Whoa! Did you hear what I just said? I didn't know that was going to be like that: joy...joy! And that would be it. I think so. I think I would really love it.*

*For a long time, I've asked myself over and over what does joy feel like? And I'm looking because I don't know. And if I don't know, I don't see how anyone else could give it to me. I never got an answer. I never got the answer until this very moment. Now I see it. I think it'll stick! Yes! But it's more than that, wait...*

*You know, I always enjoyed so much saying to people: "Come on in, I have this, I have that," also asking people if they would like to talk with each other and me...you know, and they did!...they came in, they had a*

*good time, like on my birthday....when I always have*
*had parties. Someone said to me when she read the*
*invitations for my birthday party [which Sarah gave four*
*months before she died]; "Oh, this is who you are and*
*what you do." I loved it. I said, "What are you talking*
*about?" She said, "Well, people come in, meet each*
*other. That's what you do: you get people together." I do!*
*I put people together! And it's joyful for me, huh? You*
*bet it is!*

*People have been saying that to me my whole life. And*
*I've been saying, what is that? What is it that I do?*
*I don't do anything. I can't do anything. Everybody else*
*has a skill. I don't have any skills at all. And I hate it.*
*So, I've had that conversation twenty-five times over the*
*years. Now I think I may have gotten it! That's what*
*I think, anyway.*

Maybe the next good thing wasn't ahead somewhere,
it was back *there*!! Her love of the social life had been there
all the time, a nice thing but nothing front and center;
it wasn't big enough for that. And yet it was. *"And now,"*
she said, *"we need to get this apartment so that it's not so*
*cluttered!"* Then the people could come.

## Small Things Are as Valuable as Big Ones

Who could have imagined joy could be so simple?
It wasn't success or the things in her space that would make
her happy, but to be able to do what she loved—
create and be with other people. That simple! Who knew
that people appreciated just her helping them to be human,

to come out of their shells and be together? That was a form of creativity, too.

For those activities, this space could be what it was, just less cluttered. She could still walk with Harriet. She would keep fighting not to be who she was before, but who she wanted to be now: strong enough to share time with others, have some fun, and do what she had always loved, always with people at the center. When that was no longer possible, she would be done. She could indeed "live until I'm done," if she did that.

These were all lovely things to discover, and on the other hand, so small and basic. Where were they coming from? What mystery was making this happen? Maybe the answer was *everything*. Everything that had been happening and what had not happened that she had wanted to happen. Maybe finding her roots again and the joy of having a community of tradition, not only friendships, had awakened her old feeling of being loved in some huge way. A question goes: "What do I still want that I don't have?" That question might have been relevant for Sarah a short time before. But now the question had become: "How long can I continue to do what I have always wanted to?"

Stepping out of a lifetime of habits into the deep, small mysteries of the self isn't a seamless process. The feelings are so strange that one leaves them behind, forgets them, and then runs up against them again. What seems learned and integrated into one's life one day undoes itself in the next. Anger comes and goes. The old dreams die hard. But it is out of this back and forth that the growth comes; change and resistance must mix to make the change. Otherwise, change and different feelings are always fleeting and easily fall back into old, rutted roads of thought and disappear.

In most ways, things had only changed for the worse. Sarah was sicker, and she still fell out of bed and the wait was long. But during the day she put together a new grief and loss group, attended a small discussion group on aging, and of course visited and offered herself to everyone as much as she could. She was funny. You forgot she was dying until she stood up and moved.

To an outsider, her activities might have seemed silly or trivial, but to Sarah, as she was learning, they were her life and joy—so much more so than they looked. And they weren't just hers. Dining with friends, looking for good desserts and just talking weren't only about that. They were about loving other people, showing them how to savor a life that was always brief, listening to people who were growing to need her more.

She made her signature jewelry as a creative act she could still manage even with unsteady hands and failing vision— always for others, always an expression of joy to be passed on. She made ever more wild greeting cards expressing her love in the bright colors and patterns that reflected her ebullient personality—and sent them at holidays and just for the hell of it. She visited her family often and talked on the phone with her teenage granddaughter, who also came to stay the night. Her three grandsons shared a special place in her heart, and she went to their events. She still bought clothes at thrift shops for herself and had them altered to fit her and looked for exciting finds for others. She of course developed a relationship with her seamstress, and with everyone else with whom she crossed paths. Everyone was worthy of her love and respect. And oddly, when she treated people that way, when she treated them as she wanted to be treated and showed them who she was—competent, funny, interested in them and not only demanding—life went more smoothly.

Most important and noticeable to her friends, she developed an increasing warmth and clarity about others' foibles and failures, and she forgave them more easily— sometimes seemingly effortlessly, as if she were learning to love them unconditionally. What she could give slowly became more important than what she knew or wanted for herself.

She knew she wanted to die this way, in connection with others, not alone or mentally gone. And not only for the sake of her own happiness and pride but for others. She didn't want them to remember her or her end as frightening and terrible.

People would arrive at her door after she had had another terrible night and had just enlisted help with everything she had always sworn she would do for herself forever—bathing to makeup. It would take a minute or two; then she would emerge full of smiles and open arms, genuine pleasure on her face. What detritus and struggle it had taken to get her there were left behind and kept as her own secret.

What she had said months ago became more and more real. It was not only an abstract goal but a way of life now: "When I leave this life, I want to be kind and peaceful; I don't want to be angry and afraid. So, I am trying to live that way." This was a wisdom of its own, and the rest of us absorbed it also in some way or another.

## Piecing It All Together

Sarah never had the chance to put together all the experiences of surrendering, loss of respect, going deep, and finding the importance of small things. She lived with them as experiences, not perspective. For Sarah, each change came out of significant struggle and disappointment, some form of which we will most likely face ourselves.

Sarah began to find a different way of life. She began to see that her aging and death weren't about surrender so much as about gaining respect for a process rather than an individual life. She had been forced to let some once important beliefs go, from the value of certain ideas to the nature of her contributions. But in the meantime, something else had taken over. Her vague but heartfelt recall of the language and rhythms of Jewish life and belief were life-giving. Love for others, responsibility to them, even unconditional love, all reminded her of her father, and now herself.

Joy came in friends and food shared; that bowl of spaghetti and the person sitting across from her. The wild forays to restaurants with Harriet and discussions with the wait staff at Denny's. She expanded her listening heart in every direction—and it did nothing but make her and those she listened to more aware of what mattered. It was not everything, and much was subtle. But it was enough to be worth keeping, for all of us.

This is what became Sarah's life. To be with ones she liked was close to enough. Concern for where she would go and what was "real" after this life—never a big question for her— faded even more. She had to get through death first, and meanwhile, there was also this life. She felt the simple power of caring, the importance of knowing herself, the joy of being part of something immense, and the promise, as she said, of wholeness. She seemed to be following the famous optimist Pollyanna's admonition: *"You ought to forget about dying and be glad you're living!"* Had Sarah channeled her one night? Who channels Pollyanna?

Still, it seemed that the combination not only made her happy, but others as well. It was remarkable how they all fit together.

# Chapter Eight: Leaving

*It's time.*

**Sarah Z.**

Sarah now understood completely that her condition would not improve. In the back of her mind, she had always hoped that a new cure was just around the corner, but now she knew the turn at the next block was too far away for her.

Beneath the ameliorating action of her medications, the Parkinson's had continued to progress as she aged. Now it was getting worse day by day. Her voluntary movements were increasingly hard to manage. The medications were wearing off faster. The neurotransmitter—the device in her chest that managed the brain site that stopped the Parkinson's tremors—was losing its efficacy. She was finishing her aware, active human life really, truly, and now.

Everything got harder: latching up her bra, buttoning her blouse, slipping on her pants, showering and toileting. For some, these are tolerable trade-offs for life; for Sarah, their increasingly intimate nature and her growing lack of control over her body were intolerable. This progressively compromised woman, as she saw herself, was already not who she truly was. She hated that others had to help with her private struggles. Generosity, personal responsibility, and pride were powerful dimensions of her self, and she would not surrender them easily.

Then there were the nighttime events, which did not stop but grew in frequency and length. She hardly slept at all. Of all Sarah's gifts, she felt the most precious was her mind. Without her mind and control of her thoughts, she felt she would be nothing. She could not let that happen.

She believed that when the medications ceased being effective, she would soon become a ravaged body and a totally confused and dysfunctional mind. There would be no Sarah there. That would be untenable, and she would not be able to abide it. What she had said for years about not living past the end of her *self* now was an immediate possibility and for that reason much scarier. She believed ever more strongly that no one should be made to live life in the way she was soon to experience it; nor should anyone have to see their mother, grandmother, or friend suffer in that way. If others wanted to remain alive at whatever cost, that was their call. But for her, no.

Sarah had already had a direct experience of what was ahead. A few months previously, the neurotransmitter in her chest had lost its charge. It went down and so did she. She could hardly move and felt she was indeed dying. "I've seen what it's like to not be myself," she said, "and I don't like it one bit." She feared that there would be pain at the end, and this did happen in some cases of Parkinson's. She could not manage pain, she said. It would take away all the ways she wanted to be and preoccupy her totally. Also, Sarah was candid enough to say she "just couldn't do pain." Who can?

It must be overwhelming, difficult, terribly strange, and

deeply frightening to conceive of your own end. But still, it was time to get ready to be "good to go," as some friends called it. Maybe other hopes hadn't worked out, but this one was still out there. This could be the last good thing.

Strangely, it gave her a new kind of peace to begin. She was back in control, even if it was of the end and limited by the ways her death would naturally unfold. She could still call some of the shots. That gave her a sense of clarity; she knew roughly what she had to do. She would do whatever it would take to die on her own terms while still within the law; she wanted nature to finally win, if that was what it meant. If that meant sooner rather than later, so be it.

She hoped she could manage it, prepare for it, say goodbye; she could and would finish as the woman she had made into Sarah Z.—all of her—the woman who could stop a room—and so much more. At least she would try.

I am sure none of us could fully hear or share the inner anguish of this decision and all the others she made as she moved forward—and I am sure she knew that. We are always alone in what we feel, particularly with the negative and frightening. Even if others know their own anguish and it may be similar, they do not know ours. Truly, it was easy to see her and not the disease, and while this was part of her kindness as well as her pride, it must also have made her feel that deep separation that fear and fundamentally different circumstances create between us. But perhaps that helped her see where she wanted to go more clearly.

## The Details

In the early summer of 2019, Sarah began to map out the steps that would allow her to die. She would not take her own life, but she would not live past the time her body was ready to go. She would not prolong death when she had prolonged her life as long as she could.

Sarah had been working on the problem, but from all over the map. Months earlier, notes in a caretaker's log pointed to Sarah's almost frantic search for what she should do given the results of her latest neurological exam. She asked herself:

> *What should I change in my behaviors? Exercise? Mind games? Better food plan? Ask Dr. P: is there a doctor in Vermont to contact about medically assisted dying [where it is legal in certain cases]? What about Compassion and Choices? Hospice?*

Now these questions seemed irrelevant: exercise would no longer help, she liked food, not food plans, and Vermont was too far away.

She had spent months questioning friends generally about end-of-life scenarios, discovering the very limited legal options, changing her mind from one idea to another, and repeatedly avoiding the details of any decision.

Every time she started to get some real facts, they overwhelmed and terrified her. There were so many reasons for this: what they really meant, the fear they brought up, the grief, even the looming shame and embarrassment of failure if she didn't manage to do it. And perhaps the worst of all, it was so *lonely*; who the heck had ever done this dying thing before? Okay, well, everybody, but how many had tried to die as who they were, or before they were completely gone, anyway? Those who had done it before her weren't around to ask. Maybe she could postpone matters until she was really gone and out of it. The problem was that then she might linger for a long time, or someone else would have to make the decision to end things one way or another. She couldn't leave anyone with that terrible, even possibly illegal, job. How did you do this?

Before the leap into the abyss of death itself, she had to take a Wylie Coyote leap into the canyon and look down. The plunge Wylie took always came a second or two *after* he looked. That was her situation.

Sarah was a planner and a scheduler. She kept busy every moment if she could.  So, one way to look down was to focus on the practical side of making preparations. She could set up a time frame and organize what seemed likely to be several pieces, rather than panicking about the end and letting it sweep over her slowly or quickly. She couldn't stop gravity, but maybe she could figure out how she could land. Death, too, would be planned and scheduled.

She would set matters in place that would allow her to accept the dying process in an orderly, seamless way, as much as death would allow. But she knew she didn't know enough to do this all herself. The issue wasn't just a matter of blithely saying, "I'll go when my life is done." It was a matter of the many details that had to be arranged for that to happen. Who could help lay those out with and for her?

**Getting Help**

Ellen would. A year or so before, she had met Ellen, who sometimes helped people to do this—one of a growing number of informal helpers who support those who want to die with dignity and control, legally and respectfully. They hadn't spoken for a while, but Sarah decided to enlist her help. She called. For a few weeks Ellen could not meet, but when she could, Sarah told her that she was ready to die and wanted to finalize her advance medical directive and other necessary matters. She wanted to make sure her documents and plans were tight and see about changing provisions for new medical treatments she would not want.

Being the persuasive, charming, and determined person Sarah was, she convinced Ellen to help her, but not right away. It turned out the major obstacle Ellen was concerned about was not the process, but Sarah herself. Ellen needed to make sure Sarah knew what she was doing.

Meet-ups in the warm summer months followed—in a nearby café over coffee and Cokes, and of course, snacks— or in Sarah's room. Those meetings, and others that soon followed with a number of professionals, would prove crucial to ensuring Sarah's dignified end.

At their first meeting, Ellen asked for clarity. What did Sarah want; what was she asking of her? Sarah was clear: one, living was becoming too much. She needed to help it end. And two, how could she do that? Who and what would help? Ellen dug deeper: What did she mean by "too much?" What made her want to be this intentional about her death? How about her friends and family? How would they support her if she moved ahead? Doubts—hers or theirs—could not show up later as second thoughts. This was the most final decision you could make.

As they continued to meet, Ellen continued to push her, repeating the same questions. Embedded in this discussion for both of them was the need for absolute certainty. Ellen wanted to hear that, in her words, "Sarah knew, really *knew*, what she wanted, and that her family would not challenge her decision." Sarah had no doubts: they—her daughters and her brother, her best friend, even most of her other friends, were on board. Those who strongly disagreed with her decision still knew and respected her enough to believe she was making her choice with wisdom and integrity, and in the interests of others as well as herself.

To Sarah's obvious next question—"How would she get into hospice to die?" Ellen was gently blunt: was Sarah truly intent now on following through, and did she know that actually, really, and truly meant forever? Would she be inclined at some point to leave hospice should she decide to seek treatment for something else, or try her medications again? After all, she had done this before.

Ellen explained her approach to Sarah's request in this way:

> I really wanted to know that she was solid, knew what
> she wanted, and had support. I wanted to know that she

*wasn't wavering, that she had told other people and that
it wasn't a sudden decision—things like that—and that it
all matched the advance directive that she had started
before. It couldn't be anything new. I wouldn't want to
help anyone if they had just thought about it today or
were changing their mind every week. She passed the
test.*

*Sarah was solid. She never wavered. She was committed
to moving on this. So, at the last meeting with just the
two of us, I told her, "In order to die, you have two ways
to go that we have already learned about. Now it's time
to decide. One is that you can voluntarily stop eating
and drinking when you are ready and wait for starvation
to take its course."*

This would be relatively long and hard—likely over a
month—and the question of her medications would remain.
Would they prolong the process? Would there be some sort
of adverse effects from the combination? It was also a
potentially painful process.  The other choice was better,
if still harsh: Sarah could stop her medications and turn off
her neurotransmitter.

There was no hope for her treatments now, anyway.
There was nothing to hang on for, except for the day when
she couldn't move anymore, or was completely confused.
And when would that be, and who would she be by then?
Could she decide anything by then?

On the other hand, her treatments presently gave her the
stability she still had; the literature suggested that going off

them could trigger a number of disastrous consequences before she died. Could she stand that? Neither of them knew exactly what that would entail. They would go to Sarah's next neurology appointment and ask. What would be involved if and when Sarah stopped treatment? How long would it take to die? Still, in Sarah's mind it was already decided. This was just part of the "how," not the "if."

She would make the doctor visit not just an informational meeting, but an announcement of sorts. She would determine how to set up the whole process and begin to let people know when she would begin it.

At the appointment, somewhere around 1:00 p.m. on a typical mid-summer day, Sarah, one of her daughters, her best friend, one of her beloved caregivers, Ellen, and the medical technician and physician involved in her care worked through the problem together.

Her doctor looked at all her numbers, saying, "Sarah, there's really nothing more we can do here." Her response was swift:

> Good! Because I want to stop treating this. I don't like living this way. I'm having too much difficulty.
> So, I don't want anything new, and I want to stop what we're doing. I want to be able to die, and in order to get into hospice I have to be six months terminal.

At that point, with all her medications and the neurotransmitter, she was afraid she still wasn't there yet. She could stop her medications herself, the doctor told her;

that was legal. No one could seek to prolong her life against her wish if she made her determination clear. But all her instructions about the latter had to be very detailed if she could not speak for herself.

The approach would require far more than a "Do Not Resuscitate" order, the most common protection people have against unwanted medical interventions. That could only be used if and when she stopped breathing—and it only guaranteed that she would receive no aggressive CPR. The group reviewed how an advance directive specifying no treatments for anything that might prolong her life had to include enough detail to leave no doubt about her intentions. In a serious event that might require hospitalization, she would have to be explicit about no treatment at all, even for something unrelated to the Parkinson's or her medications, even small interventions like liquids or antibiotics.

In other words, did she understand that if a heart attack or stroke or something else made her unable to speak—had she made it made it absolutely clear that her agent (the person or persons she designated to speak for her) must be prepared to say that she wished no treatments for anything that would perhaps prolong her life?

Yes, it was true: even a short time without her medications would likely seriously compromise Sarah. The effects of going off the Parkinson's medications could increase her suffering in recognized ways, including the possibility of pneumonia. Her symptoms would be uncontrolled, and the dyskinesia, the involuntary, erratic movements that the medications had ameliorated, would increase. She likely wouldn't be able to communicate or express herself clearly. She didn't want people to see her like that.

How long would it take to die if she stopped her medications? She knew that once she stopped her treatments, she would no longer be able to eat or drink normally. She wanted to refuse all other forms of feeding, nutrition, and hydration. The doctor didn't know for sure as everyone was different, but given no water, Sarah likely would not manage more than three to four days. Maybe less, maybe more. Not much more. But what if it did take more? When could hospice be called? For that, the doctor said, they would have to ask hospice.

It was not ideal. But what other options were there that didn't involve some illegal action? Her state had no "medical support in dying" provisions of any kind. She was angry; how could a state condone torture? Because that was what it would be. But okay. It was too late for her to fight that battle.

The discussion didn't have much farther to go. If she truly was ready to go ahead with this and free herself, as she saw it, then the best and quickest option would indeed be to stop her medications and turn off her neurotransmitter. She would then be unable to eat or drink, and death would follow naturally, in what seemed to be a shorter time than doing anything else that was legal might take.

Sarah and Ellen next met to discuss hospice care. As Ellen

recounted: "I was trying to get the two pieces connected. When Sarah stopped treatment, when could she get into hospice care? There would be a gap." And that gap would be terrible, they knew. Ellen, continuing to make all the connections as tight as she could, met with Sarah and the hospice nurse practitioner in Sarah's room. The nurse practitioner knew Sarah from her entry and exit into hospice care the year before; Sarah, still well dressed and made up, still in control, gave her pause.

Ellen wanted to be sure Sarah was still clear on her decision, and that the nurse practitioner would hear her apparent determination; Ellen never stopped giving Sarah chances to change her mind. She told Sarah: "The reality now is that either you're dying or you're not. Are you sure you're ready?"

The nurse practitioner was even-handed and polite, but she told them what they already knew, and firmly; "To get into hospice care, Sarah, you have to be terminally ill, with six months or less to live."

Ellen had figured this would come up. She made it clear that everyone there understood why Sarah had been discharged from hospice the last time; it was because she was considering a curative treatment for something, and also because she really was not within six months of dying on her maintenance medications. This time she had a plan to go off treatment. The question was, how soon could she get into hospice when she stopped her treatment? Ellen reflected:

*That was what the hospice nurse practitioner needed to hear. She was great, and very clear: "When you stop your treatment—the minute you're not taking your meds and turn off your transmitter—we can admit you to hospice that same day. We will be here at your room with hospice care—with the meds and comfort care that you'll need."*

That was it. Given what she knew, that's what Sarah was most afraid of—coming off treatment and waiting to be admitted to hospice. Ellen said:

*It was such a critical piece. People wait too long, and they don't get the doctor, the hospital, and the residential facility all on board soon enough. Then everybody is trying to set things in motion, make decisions, and prevent useless interventions and it gets very disorganized. So, we did that way before.*

*Now, if all went as planned, Sarah would discontinue her treatment, notify hospice, and go into care immediately. That way, any pain could be managed, her body could be stilled, and her mind would be as clear as it could be. Her body would be free to take its natural course.*

*Then Sarah and I met in her room and we talked again about being ready, really ready. When did she want to do this? Because when you do it, you're doing it.*

There would be no going back on her medications and the neurotransmitter; there was no guarantee that they would work once stopped, and they likely would not. Yes. She was ready.

Now, Ellen told Sarah, it was important to think about a time. Setting a time makes it even clearer to someone thinking about such a move just how real the decision is and whether it can finally be made or not. Sarah sat for a bit and asked about hospice again. Ellen assured her:

> We have the info, and we know that when you go off all
> of this, you can be admitted to hospice. But you have to
> decide when you want to do it so you can let people
> know and finish the things you want to finish.

Good point, that, about finishing things and letting people know. Ellen:

> Sarah decided then that she would do it, but she would
> wait until her best friend, who had come to her
> appointments for years and knew what Sarah wanted,
> returned from a long-planned trip to Europe. She said:
> "I don't want to do it before she goes, because I don't
> want her to be all sad, so I'll do it when she gets back.
> Besides, she said she would kill me if I died while she
> was in Europe."

> So, she put a date on the calendar not too long after her
> friend's return. I told her she would need to talk to her
> family and be sure they were all still on board, now that
> it was getting real. I asked: "Is there anyone you want to
> have visit? Is there anything you want to do?" So, we
> just talked about tying up the loose ends. She said she
> was going to finish her life around Yom Kippur.

146

Over the next weeks, a few of those back-and-forth moments still surfaced in Sarah's mind, as they would in anyone's. She wondered if she would be able to do it. She asked her dear friend if perhaps they should have a code word that would mean "stop." Sarah would say it and her friend would call everything off. The friend said, "No. No code word. You've been planning this for years and years. You're ready. This is what you want. You will do it. I know you will. You don't need a code word. You would hate that."

Indeed, there was no code word, and no change of heart. "I am so proud of you," her friend said later at Sarah's deathbed; "you're doing it just the way you wanted to."

Sarah set the date for mid-September and started letting people know. There was time; a month, and she felt pretty good right then. She would tell people in stages.

Now Sarah, her best friend, and Ellen thought they were all set, and Sarah could catch her breath. She could start saying her goodbyes, soak up the last sounds of restaurant happiness, and the last laughs. She could eat the last bowls of spaghetti and the last yummy desserts, and give all the love she had to all the many people she had found she loved—and who loved her. She could take in their love for her without, she hoped, any second thoughts. She could explain things to them that she had figured out in the course of making her decision—and maybe in the course of her life.

Matters took an unexpected turn, which should not have surprised anyone, but did. Sarah contracted a gastrointestinal infection the month before her planned departure. She went to the ER; by the time she arrived, only the neurotransmitter to her brain was working, the medications having worn off between the time she became ill, was found—a matter of an unknown period of time on the floor again—and arrived at the hospital. The pain of watching her quick decline was immense for everyone.

With both daughters' agreement, her written advance medical directive and her own voice, she said clearly, "No treatment." The doctors demurred. This was a small matter of some hydration to replace lost fluids and perhaps an antibiotic. Wouldn't she rather have some fluids and come back? This didn't have to kill her; she just had a stomach bug.

Sarah's daughters were distraught but accepting of their mother's decision, as they had promised to be. Her best friend supported them by phone. Ellen was watching; she heard Sarah say very clearly, "No, this is my chance; this is my opportunity. Why wait? It's time."

She would have to turn off the neurotransmitter herself. No one else could do it; that would be a crime. The end was happening with the groundwork of goodbyes unfinished. But that was the way death was offering her an ending she knew she could manage and had the courage to take on.

She turned off the neurotransmitter, her daughters by her side.

It was early evening, and some half hour and worlds away I was checking out of the grocery store. A little later that night, hospice took over Sarah's care. The next morning,

Catherine and I went to the nursing facility. She had wanted to "live until I'm really done," and she had done it, and she had also known when to say "enough."

On the last night she lay dying, to those by her bedside it seemed that in her mind she was not lying down at all. She was holding a party. You can imagine it—folks dancing, glasses clinking, the songs people knew, happy guests standing in clutches talking about important things. It was all *fun*, a "hooray, we are all here *together*," a Sarah event, when she was happiest. The night before, she had been dreaming of partying too, asking people not to dance on the tables, laughing as she always did, with her hands. Cake was involved. This night her body was mostly quiet...but clearly not her mind.

Remember back. In her last months, when she dared to sleep, she had found herself struggling with a recurring delusion: she had to get to a most important wedding— so important, yet so elusive. She was missing it, didn't know where it was, nor even whose wedding it was. It undid her, this wedding, and not being able to find it was nearly intolerable.

The delusions, more real than her life, came often. They fooled her with trains not to the wedding but to nowhere, and then transformed the trains into the hallways of her assisted living facility. Somehow, she found she had been left in a parking lot nowhere near the wedding. Another night she arrived late, only to find no one there. Everyone had gone home. Her waking-life aides said, as if they knew, "no wedding here," and "go back to bed." She had, studying the walls for clues of where she was. It seemed again and again that there was no wedding, and would not be.

But maybe she had not been wrong. Toward the end of that last night perhaps the train arrived; those sterile, silent halls gave way to rooms alive with music and voice; and people she knew came rushing to greet her almost giddily. That night, no one can say she did not eat cake to her heart's content, laugh with her head thrown back, hug the breath out of people, and dance the night away. Even if it is only our dream for her now, at least one person in the world believes that on that last night, maybe not far from morning, she found her wedding.

# Chapter Nine:
# Sarah's Window—A Practical
# Way of Aging

*We shouldn't ask how to stay young, but how*
*we can learn to become old.*

### Roberta Culbertson

*In this short life that only lasts an hour*
*How much – how little – is within our power*

### Emily Dickinson (1292)

It is likely that you have many questions about Sarah's struggles, from how she prepared for and addressed them to how they pertain to your own situation. You may even wonder why she made such a big deal of some of them. Whatever your questions, it is hard to just swim around in the whole soup of them, bumping into different issues at different times: a carrot of simplifying here and a parsnip of going deep there.

She had said, "Tell them this," many, many times, as she discovered one problem after another, from the repeated need to give up what she loved to the hundred ways she felt considered useless. Then, to her surprise, among those difficult things she wanted to tell she began to add in ever greater measure the quiet ways in which those problems and others were easing and sometimes falling away.

You will remember that Catherine and I visited Sarah often and listened to what she told us. As we watched her end unfold, we tried to make sense of it in a way that allowed us to think about her admonitions to us and others. We looked for ways of seeing the different elements of her struggle and how to think about them now, while many of her immediate problems were still our future ones.

In listening to and then telling Sarah's story, we saw her journey fall naturally into four significant challenges. She responded to each of these in ways uniquely her own. The ways she did so have made up the chapters of this book thus far, and they have brought us to this point.

First, there were her herculean efforts to keep what had been important to her, and to contribute to a world that did not want or expect her to. But two other challenges lay buried beneath these: how to go deep into herself, and then how to accept herself and others as they were. These latter two allowed her to go back and slowly accept the need to simplify, and to adopt new, almost unrecognized, ways of contributing to a world that now needed something else from her.

As she loosened the knots on her past and her dreams, another Sarah began to emerge alongside the one we had known; one with even greater inner depth, some true comfort, and a joy that shone in her deeper expression and acceptance of love. In the end, perhaps culminating in her dying dreams, she found she belonged— what greater vision of that than the ineffable, moving, rich experience of a wedding? Why not dance?

It can be useful to have a framework that emphasizes what she might have avoided, rather than what she encountered. Something that might look at how she could have found the answers she did sooner rather than later.

This chapter introduces a structure, or model, that offers a holistic way to think about aging in a practical and personalized way based on each person's own values, beliefs, and dreams. We can use this model, called Sarah's Window, to structure our own preparations for aging within our own circumstances. It offers a way to develop a broad approach that can help to shape planning now and make decisions when the time comes.

The exciting thing about using a model such as this idea of a Window is that it can lead us to develop a more proactive way of life that is attentive to aging and our values and ideas about it. It can help us take an open view of what is coming and be clear about what we bring from our experience to face it. It can help us prepare more fully than Sarah did, all the way down to the smallest details that matter to us.

Sarah managed to find her way to a deeper understanding of her life and a way to leave the earth as she had wanted: happier than she had been, kind, and with some peace, whatever that last might have meant to her. You might say that the end of her life became a window onto herself and what was important to her and others. She was not afraid of death, and at the end she danced at a wedding she had tried to find for a long time. We don't know whose wedding it was, but she found a happiness there that had eluded her. It is easy to believe that wherever she may be now, it is not likely painful or lonely. It might even be her idea of heaven.

Sarah wanted people to take from her detailed story what they could use. She had said over and over, "don't wait"— don't wait to find out what she had learned by hard lessons or to prepare for the problems she had not expected. Don't do it as she had, struggling to adapt to a set of circumstances that in earlier years she could never have anticipated. Don't think you have it all sewed up, for the devil—and the divine—are in the details.

**Sarah's Window**

Put together, Sarah's struggles offer a window on getting old. Looking through it, we see the time lost, the hard lessons learned, and the long process of coming to clarity about what is happening. But if that perspective can be turned around, maybe it can become action rather than response—the future rather than the past. It might suggest a way to grow up and into aging and dying in a less painful way.

Like a window with four panes, Sarah's discoveries were: the need to simplify; contribute; go deep; and care and connect. These categories emerged naturally from her experiences.

Sarah's Window (or the Window) is a way to start keeping track of what we think about, value, and ignore, and how looking at how one's day-to-day self gives clues and ideas about how to navigate what will likely be a long way to the end of life.

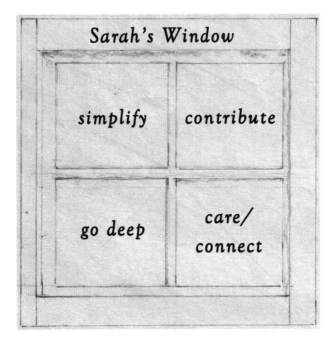

### The Purpose of the Window

How will you live through the changes that come to you as you grow older? Though they will not be Sarah's exactly, they will still involve having to give up things and identities all the way to death itself. If you are unprepared, these changes may confront you with a sense of powerlessness and even uselessness and resentment as you enter your frail years. Unexpected events or debilitation may threaten to strip away much of who you are, and you will have to find what is left of you or be hollowed out by circumstances. And finally, people you love will have to care for you; you will need to open the gates to your compassion to find new, simpler ways of caring and supporting them also. It sounds grim, and it can be. When it is not grim, it is often because people have taken steps like these to prepare.

The Window offers ways to define and take such steps with a bit of structure, and before the issues become too bleak or unmanageable. Some of the future we clearly cannot control. But as when a storm is coming, if we look out the window, we can prepare for it.

Using the Window as described below, you can see ways to simplify your life, offer wisdom to others, dig into your deepest values, and maintain connections throughout your aging life, and even to your decisions about dying. You can create a holistic picture of your aging, integrating the steps you must take with the ones that will enrich you and those around you.

Sarah's Window is a model that can lead us to different ways of seeing our own time unfolding just beyond or behind the present. It can expand the present forward into planning and backwards into our original selves and dreams, which in fact already shape how we are aging.

Life will still work out differently than we expected. We will have to roll with the facts and make our decisions even when we are confronted with only unsatisfactory choices. But if we know our own values and beliefs, have made the changes to our lives that will simplify what we need and allow us to keep giving, we will be able to make choices that suit us. If we have learned how to play the guitar or dance to the tunes in advance, the music will be meaningful and perhaps even enjoyable.

## The Four Panes

If we see Sarah's Window as having four panes, we can look through each one and see our world in a particular way. We can turn Sarah's discoveries on their head.

Now, this may seem a simplistic thing to do: put all those struggles into something as concrete as a window? How can that help? But the brain works well with metaphors. They help it organize and retain ideas. An image like a window actually helps to anchor many concepts and give a focus to problems. It is a mnemonic device that keeps the ideas in front of us by representing them as part of a common object. If we can conjure up an image of a window, we might remember what is in it. Medieval monks used to remember long texts in this way; they imagined a castle and put different ideas in different rooms.

The four panes, in this case, point to anticipation rather than capitulation: simplify rather than have to surrender, contribute rather than accept powerlessness, go deep rather than feel defeated, and care and connect rather than retreat.

In short, they are *simplify, contribute, go deep, and care and connect*. These too, distilled to this level, may seem trivial and obvious, but each one can take a lifetime to fill in, unpack and use. They are like the old game "Go," which had the tag line, "a minute to learn, a lifetime to master."

## The Meanings of the Panes

If we look into each pane a bit more deeply, we can see what each one offers in the way of ideas and questions about our own aging. The meaning of each pane and the reasons behind it are relatively easy to lay out. After that, we can look at how to use the panes as tools for thinking. Each pane will sound familiar from Sarah's story. But now the point is to shine the light forward onto your own life.

### 1. Simplify

Sarah was prepared neither for the degree of simplification her aging would require nor the decisions about giving up that she would have to make. Most of us complicate our lives by accumulating more than we can manage: things, ideas, friends, lovers, projects and commitments. We may see them as measures of our worth and essential to who we are. But as we change, needs change, and the ability to manage all we used to manage lessens. If we are to serve others and not ruin our own chances at wholeness, we must cut back on things that we cannot do or that make us sick, clutter our homes, or tie us down. And we must continue to cut back as long as we must, lessening our load like explorers trekking across ice for weeks and eventually even abandoning precious specimens and valued rocks if they are to get home again.

Interesting questions immediately begin to pop up in Sarah's Window. What to cut back first? And what barriers immediately appear? Why is it hard? How might you do it in a way that suits you, and what do you have to think about? There will be not only your first move, but others will likely follow. Or if not moving, how will you do as much cleaning and sorting as possible to more easily navigate your house without falling, and free your children or some other executor of your estate, meager or not, from a long and tedious job of cleaning out when you die? How will you leave your finances, so the debt is minimal and the records in order? How will you set up bed and bath so you can shower and get to the toilet, and what will you do when those become impossible? Do you want to leave it to others to help, and if so, will you be able to pay them, or help them in turn? It is critical to remember that the whole issue of simplifying isn't only about the next few years; it is about all the way to the end.

Even good works may have to be reduced to what you have the energy to do. This is especially maddening. But exhaustion makes one more ego-centered and resentful. When we feel martyred, we don't feel happy, and no one else is happy because we moan about how we are trying to make them so from our empty well of old bones and tiredness. It is also possible to try to help in ways that put you in danger: climbing the ladder to the attic to get down the Christmas decorations, carrying your own forty-pound suitcase. Decline is the natural consequence of aging, so it might be useful to think of how you can do less that will feel like more. You can be helpful while you can, to build up "credit," as it were, for help you will need later. Helping now for later help is the way of poor communities. Accepting necessary help is also. No one is an island, young or old. But it takes work and thinking rationally.

We are told how important it is to stay active, and this is

very true. A key to longevity is keeping the body and mind moving. But you have to simplify what you do and then keep doing it, changing as your body changes. Maybe take lessons in learning to fall safely, or how to move with minimal pressure on your joints. Try chair yoga, balance classes, or walking (yes, it is boring for some of us). Find other ways that save your body while keeping you moving. Ride the racing bike as long as you can. Accept when you cannot and do something else. If you fall or have a heart attack because you are too proud or driven or become unable to do much just because it is "too hard," you will eventually complicate everyone's life, including your own. Stop mowing the lawn and lifting heavy bags, but keep weeding, maybe. This is a form of simplifying, too.

Stepping back and cutting down can seem strange, and strangely empty. Friends may get hurt, the family may be confused or offended, and meals at home might become simpler. There may be blank spaces on the windowsill where some knick-knacks used to be, or an empty corner. Maybe there will be more time, and less to fill it.

But gaining *time* is a major benefit of all simplification: it lightens the material and mental loads we carry and will eventually pass on to others if we don't set them aside.

If we can sit long enough in the silence to find in the quiet spaces something larger and more fulfilling, if we can just *relax*, we can do what the elderly are supposed to do. To know this and experience it becomes the best gift or service you can offer yourself and others. You may see how little all the stuff mattered; how much you can demonstrate about life just from the example of being a little calmer and a little less cluttered. A few months of living after simplifying something—anything—will likely show how any voluntary surrender is in fact a real source of freedom. Maybe grief or regret too, but also some degree of release.

How can you do this? To make the changes real before they need to make them, some people have the courage to imagine what it will be like to surrender the car keys by trying to manage without the car while they can still drive. You might be able to imagine what it will be like not to be able to see or hear by briefly taking your cell phone from yourself, or the television, or books. Working in a long-term care facility, I find I have to imagine less and less of what to do. I see what matters to me. How painful it is to see the losses; how I wonder what they will feel like to me. My only option haunts me: how can I prepare for what I can't fully anticipate? But I need to try to prepare for what is most likely and what I can at least partly control—for everyone's sake. I need to be able to see what may happen whatever I do, and be prepared not to fight the inevitable but learn to see what it may teach.

With any information like this about yourself, you could think now about simplifying in more concrete ways. Then you would be able to integrate your ideas on this with the other panes of the Window to get a full picture of how you might want to negotiate your future.

Using the *simplify* window pane then, would entail

thinking about what *cutting back* would mean for you, how you might do it, and how you could make it a part of your whole aging process. It would also entail getting your business affairs in order and putting aside the money you can for your aging. This can save others a great deal of trouble later and will make it easier for you to follow your money and use it wisely as working with numbers gets harder. You might also find the ultimate benefit: needing less means you will be able to be less pained by loss, and more able to support yourself however long you may live, and gentler on others who care about you and will care for you.

More on how you might frame and use this perspective follows in the next sections, but let's continue with the next panes for now.

## 2. Contribute

We know from neuroscience that humans are neurologically and psychologically configured to help one another. If we weren't, the species would long be extinct, for we are too puny to manage on our own. Scientists confirm that we are cellularly and hormonally programmed to reach out to one another and to share. Over millennia these truths have been integrated into the tenets of nearly all societies as respect, generosity, kindness, tolerance, and of course, love. Laws and shared values must support these because they counter an equally necessary and strong imperative: the individual body's neurological and hormonal structures of self-protection. The pull of bodily safety is very powerful, and so many means of creating togetherness are critical to balance it.

The aging are an important part of this network of human cooperation, and are left out at a society's peril. They can grasp the role of the community better than others, partly because they are losing their ability to fight or care for themselves and see the value of being with others. By virtue of simplifying, they also have more time to reflect on what is important about life, finding that the answer is often what happens in peace rather than war, and cooperation rather than fighting.

Counter to modern attitudes about the elderly, older people have an evolutionary obligation to carry forward and share the deep human knowledge it took them a lifetime to learn. They hold and work the knitting needles of a culture. They re-knit lives and values, broken hearts, and happiness. In many cultures, the old are the judges and the peacemakers. Maybe they can't do this all the way to the very end of their lives, but in this age and culture we age slowly, and so we have even longer to fulfill this imperative before we become too old. Sarah saw this when she decided to contribute to this book, and to think of it as her legacy. It was most important to her as she could do less and less; it was a contribution to others, and would be a link to them long after she had passed.

The young actually *want* us to take on this role; they are angry not when we try, but when we don't—or deliver our messages in ways that belittle them. However much skill and technical ability a younger person may have, everyone still feels the first stomach-drop of rejection, gets confused about love, and may someday be unsure how to tell right from wrong.

We know how those experiences were for us. We can learn more still if we look inward and backward to our own struggles. We can sit down and say how love was for us, and how we have wrestled through questions of right, wrong, and in-between. Continuing the species relies on some members retaining and passing on values and meaning. Older brains are configured to do that by slowing the mind and body down in some active and self-serving areas and opening the mind in others as part of the aging process.

Yet this job of the elderly in modern times is often taken from them. Sarah found that it may be difficult for others to accept the contributions of people whom they consider past their prime. But that doesn't mean we can't prove them wrong.

Doing whatever we can in commitment to others enhances everyone's happiness, including our own. It can even contribute to the planet that sustains us all. What people do in love and openness loosens the tightness and anxiety that make life so fearsome. It also opens the door to reciprocity, which as we age, we need more and more.

Catherine and I see some people in the facility in which we work keeping going despite serious health problems. Some make me ashamed of my complaints about being tired as they show how to accept never walking again, losing short-term memory, or knowing they will soon die. They tell us all kinds of things that help, including their stories of their own years, which always reflect what they still love and value. They take on activities with others even when these are not to their liking, just to keep the circle of community alive. Most poignantly, many remind us that family and friends are the most precious part of any life and that ties broken there, or connections limited by distance, are the deepest wounds of all. A few people manage to smile just because they are kind; it is what they offer for our own willingness to sit and learn. Together we satisfy one another's evolutionary need to be useful.

Contributing needn't be anything great, as Sarah found. But we all have something to give and that doesn't stop just because we are old. The *contribute* window pane focuses the mind on these possibilities. It also allows us to think about why people might get frustrated with people who demand what they must but forget that they can offer also.

### 3. Go Deep

Contributing is enriched by our own self-understanding, and simplifying is made easier by knowing what we value and need. Every one of us has a deep well of knowledge we don't often use. Simplifying, the quiet confidence that comes from slowing down, and the sweet satisfaction that comes from helping others as they need it ease our outer life and may let deeper and older parts bubble up. We may find room to look beyond our everyday craziness to what is inside. Some memories or regrets are hard, and maybe should be left alone. But not all of what we have stored in our minds over a lifetime turns out to be as dark or slimy as many people fear. At least some of it can turn out to be crystal clear and cool, and can quench all kinds of thirst.

For Sarah, going deep was all but forced upon her, though she had always been a thinker. It required giving up getting what she wanted and seeing how other people suffered by her actions. It involved looking back to her past and finding a place she belonged. In her own way, she found her own version of faith there.

Going deep can be about looking more deeply into the stories people tell about themselves and others, and the stories we tell about ourselves. It can involve trying to remember what love feels like or remembering that everyone is as scared as you are. It is illuminating and freeing to sit sometimes and let the things that frighten you the most have some space in your thoughts and ask; "Why? What am I afraid of? That I am a bad person? That I am evil? That I am stupid? That other people will hurt me? Why do I think these thoughts at all? The process can go as deep as you wish, but at some point, like magic, the whole edifice of a particular fear or even regret or anger may begin to crumble, or at least some turrets and walls may fall. Sometimes the greatest suffering comes from resisting what doesn't seem bearable to know or from opening up its outside layers over and over again. If you rip off a Band-Aid time and again and dig around in the wound, it doesn't heal. If you treat it gently and clean and care for it, it does. If you are easier with your quieter self, it can be possible to turn toward the suffering and just say; "Okay, what do you want or what do I want from you?"

At the same time, if you ask yourself what makes you happy, you can take your mind in a different direction and find sources of happiness and even depth, as Sarah did when she recalled being in the synagogue with her father. Then, following that path of memory and old questions can bring another kind of wisdom, or another bit of life, maybe even a happy one after a lifetime of revisited suffering.

Going deep in these ways, asking some personal questions and trying not to fear or refuse the answers, appreciating emerging chances for happiness, is one way to work with the Window. What might it unveil not only about yourself, but about what that self will need and be able to offer as you age? How might it make simplifying easier, or suggest something to contribute to others?

The window pane of going deep can help uncover and open the door to a last chance to become or find whatever dreams are still inside, or to understand why they are still there. Opening those old, overstuffed file drawers of the mind and laying out the facts and feelings can make it possible to let certain unrequited loves go, or to forgive oneself for something unforgiveable by finally accepting responsibility for it.

Going deep can also lead to more metaphysical, spiritual, or religious questions. Moving past one's own personal struggles can lead to deeper questions about the world and life itself, or they may have been there your whole life. This is the window pane that lets you explore what you feel and wonder about the existence of God, life after death, the meaning of a life, and more. These are critical questions for some, not so much for others. But as death nears, they may become more critical to anyone, and then it is good to take the time to pursue them. There are many interesting phenomena at death that often belie a scientific view of it.

As they lie dying, many things people did not care about or believe suddenly become important. For others, what they have dearly believed for a lifetime may desert them. Where is God? He was always there and now he is gone. People mock the idea of seeing one's dear departed on the other side until on their own deathbed they see them. Lying in the dark and wondering why you, why now, is a lonely place, as is finally fearing the emptiness that threatens on the other side. What if Hell is real? Some try to look at what is coming, and sometimes it seems they see it. It is painful to see the people around the deathbed crying should you begin to sense you will be okay but cannot summon the energy to tell them. What will happen after you die? Will you mourn for those you left behind? Will you be able to tell the people you love that you are okay? Or will you be a bit of ash floating down a stream as everyone waves goodbye? Do the questions, much less the answers, matter to you?

What if you thought about these matters before, and tried to imagine what dying itself, not just aging, might mean or feel, or how your death might matter to others? I have seen people full of fear or anger at the end, or comatose. Might they have been missing the last, great experience of life?

Maybe it's possible to examine deeply the incompleteness, anger, fear, or even the desire to finally go that might accompany your death, before you face the end itself. Could you know and believe in some view of dying and death if you had thought about it for a long time by then? What if it were helpful to those around you to know you were at peace, rather than afraid or enraged?

### 4. Care and Connect

Going deep is about looking into *yourself*, understanding what you are, and why you feel as you do. It can also be about finding some faith or philosophy to live by, from a religion to the wholeness of nature, or a commitment to giving and loving in a meaningless universe. Finally, it may set you to looking at the unfathomable matters of dying and death in ways that will serve you and others. Caring and connecting, on the other hand, are about expanding your *horizons*, not yourself.

At the end of her life, Sarah was full of caring, and she wanted to connect with everything—from other people to a plate of spaghetti. She still had worries and fears, and she was facing death. But she also was having a good time while carrying all of that. She loved people, loved what she did, and kept being useful, even while she faced death day after day.

Maybe it isn't surprising that she grew outwardly as well as

inwardly; love, caring, and the importance of connection get lost in the everyday hubbub of getting things done or caring for all we have and think we need. Focusing on the ways in which we were wronged and how we feel useless also takes away from the imperative now of reaching out to others.
In contributing, being with others is the *duty* of the aging; caring and connecting are about the *joy* of aging. It is about recognizing how short our time is and how much there is to do and feel in that tiny remaining instant. That can make life precious and full, rather than tedious and fearful.
It is a way to open back up to life, often just in time.

Caring and connecting, as Sarah saw it, is something that comes fully only to the degree that you can let go of protecting who you believe you must be. It seems to take letting go of anguish about what is being lost, and trying to expand our appreciation for what we are not losing just yet.

Sarah's experience shows us that once she had begun to accept her death and relax into her limited power over it and also over her life, she was freed up to care more. She didn't need to be anyone special because she wasn't. She could hold hands with everyone.

That is the benefit of looking for ways to care and connect, and the purpose of this window pane is to let us stop trivializing these ways of being and make time for them, and also seeing that letting go of our expectations of others is actually freeing.

There really is no difference between us all; we are all equally scared. And all the while, beyond us, there is the universe or God or love or just what is, ticking along, holding us in its embrace and throwing away our mistakes. Maybe at the end it is possible to care and connect because we begin to see that we are all stardust and light.

### Working With the Window

The four matters or perspectives the Window can help to explore may seem daunting or way deeper than you ever want to go, and maybe this approach isn't for you. But getting started is easy, and whether the work will have meaning and use for you will quickly become evident.

As they say, "it doesn't work unless you work it." Sarah's Window is something to do and keep doing somewhat regularly, or when a problem comes up. It is a way to focus and organize your thoughts so you can consciously watch what you do and think, or don't do and think, and see what is important to you. It also keeps you balanced so you don't emphasize one concern over others, and then perhaps wonder why you are stuck there.

Using the Window begins with drawing the image of a window, then compiling a list related to the window panes, or if you prefer, writing what might be on the list directly on the panes. From time to time, you can look at what you have written to get a full picture of what you are currently feeling, doing, and seeing. All of this helps you to keep moving along, accepting changes, resisting when necessary, and learning and working through new issues that come. That's it. Perhaps it is obvious that the earlier you start, the better, because you will have more time to prepare for the parts that will be most difficult.

## The Basics

It might be useful before you start to work with the Window itself to make a list of what matters concern you about your aging. Are you afraid of getting sick? Why? Are you concerned about the money it will cost to keep going? What about losing your mind to a form of dementia? Perhaps you are afraid you will die overwhelmed and exhausted from caregiving even before the one you care for dies. Maybe you are wondering what the point of life has been and what more you should have done. Or what you can do now to remain vital and healthy.

This list of your concerns is just a first step, and not part of the Window, which is more about working positively along particular lines than worrying about a future that will head off in its own direction whatever we do. The point of working with the Window is to get you ready to go with what is needed and adjust to what must be.

So, after you do this and have become thoroughly scared and unnerved and think the whole idea of the Window is stupid, you will be in a good place to begin to use the Window.

## 1. Start Working the Panes

Set aside some time for the task; maybe a half hour to an hour. Get a notebook or a piece of paper. Draw your window—as simple as a square. Divide it into four "panes."

Imagine this window is your life. If you need a boost to get started, write the following question by each pane:

**First Pane:**

What can I do to simplify my life? What will be difficult? Why?

**Second Pane:**

How can I contribute to my family and others? How can I still help?

**Third Pane:**

What do I really want to know about my life? Can I go deeper? Do I want to?

**Fourth Pane:**

How can I best care for myself and others, maybe giving up on some of my ideas about myself?

And finally, what is a good balance for me among these four? Which do I care most about, or which am I neglecting now?

If you want, you can add to the end of each of these questions, "right now." Or you can skip these questions and ask your own that have to do with the same four topics of the Window. Once you start playing with your ideas for each pane, they will likely come quickly. List them, as they come, in the panes themselves, in a notebook, or wherever.

## 2. Make a List of What You Bring to the Work

So, you have your list of what is important to you and what work it will take. But with what? It's easy to assume you have nothing to bring to this complicated, ongoing process. But everyone has some good traits and strengths that are relevant. It might seem like those are fading with age, but the basic qualities that underlie them remain. Maybe you loved running. Now your knees are shot or there is nowhere to run, or you get winded or have heart problems. You may not be able to run, but you still have a lot that made it possible to be a good runner: you know how to push through; you have discipline; you know what feels good about working hard; you have memories; you know what your shoes sound like on pavement and gravel and how that is almost dreamlike sometimes. You know what it feels like to have it all under control—body, mind, terrain. Maybe you know the near ecstasy of seeing the sky as you crest a long hill, or the camaraderie that comes from friends next to you on a long run.

Maybe you like to do other things: read, play with your dog or your cat or the parrot, swim, lie in the sun, visit your kids and grandkids, nieces and nephews, and others. Maybe your best evening is going to a play or eating out. It doesn't matter, because each activity gives you something to keep, and that, whatever it is, will continue even after the activities themselves are no longer possible. Just look for a moment: if you read, you know how to imagine and understand what someone you never met wants to tell you. If you like to eat out, you know the joys of food and how it warms people to one another, soothes the body and increases happiness and good feeling. You know that eating can be a source of joy. So, you know joy, too.

Make a list of all you know you have to offer to yourself and others, all the insight you already have that can be useful in considering each pane of the Window. Often it seems like nothing, but look again. Can you cook a good scrambled egg? It takes a lot to do that. A good scrambled egg is a work of art. Can you have the patience to watch a child try to put a square block in a round hole and not tell her it won't fit? Can you just sit still? We are full of skills and gifts that we will need as we age and death comes near, though we hardly call them that. Might as well get them out and dust them off now.

You can put these items on another list, or wherever you think they might fit with the window panes. Or draw another window and put them there. The whole thing is flexible. It is a process, not a program.

### 3. List What You Can Do Next

As you address each of these four perspectives, make lists of what you think you could do for each one now—things to go and try today. Put your skills and abilities together with the perspectives the Window provides. Maybe you had to prepare for a race once, or maybe you've read a book about aging. Use these to work with the actions and perspectives the Window suggests. But don't get carried away. This is like exercising to the point of exhaustion one day because you have just started and feel so behind. But by the next day your body rebels against being pushed that hard and soon it all falls apart.

## 4. Do Something

A list is nice, but the Window is about doing things that help. Start doing or considering some items on your list. Don't overwhelm yourself. Start small, with one or two things, maybe only in one pane at a time. Or take an idea and work it through all the panes. Try out what you wrote about. Write out the results. Try something else.

Don't set yourself up by setting impossible goals for your own personality. There is no point in deciding today to be kind to everyone. Just start with not being rude, maybe, to one or two people who irritate you. That might fall into the going deep pane. Maybe you need to heal some old, battered relationships. Why? How will you start? What can you bring to the effort? Maybe you can look up the person's address today. Maybe you could finally take that bag of clothes that has sat on the floor for six months to the thrift shop this week. Or maybe you could get a book on aging from the resources section in the back of this book or somewhere else, and start getting some of the facts on what happens with aging.

Be sure to notice what changes you feel as you do something before you forget them. You will likely be amazed by how soon just making a step toward some degree of mindful work and thought about likely the biggest issue in your life for the next ten to twenty years makes everything a little lighter. Changes may come that don't seem related at all to what you did, but they likely will be.

Over time, you can revisit the things on your list. Some day, push yourself a little and think ahead; imagine what you can do in the way of contributing to life when you begin to fail and can't do what you do now. What can a frail person do is one question; but what will *you* want to do, or be able to do? What can you offer when you can no longer drive? This is a more productive approach than being angry that your kids took away your keys.

My mother-in-law had a list of people she called every morning from her bed, for example, to make sure they were all right, check in and offer a friendly voice. She didn't get up until noon, and rarely left her place. But she was happy to have a purpose, and a circle of friends in the bargain.

With time, it will likely become evident that any act of simplifying, generosity, self-reflection, or kindness bears fruit in some way, though you may not make the connection immediately. Something about living in the alternative, attentive way that emerges from the Window begins to change neural pathways, not in the form of great moments of awareness, but in subtle, behavioral ways. "Wow, I didn't fly off the handle that time like I usually do. Just didn't feel the need." Next time you might fly off again, but some new neural line has still been laid down next to the old one. Maybe it will be that one that triggers first next time. Maybe you can encourage it by trying to remember it. Maybe it will loosen some knot.

### A Toolbox for Using the Window

Taking on any new activity that engages the mind,

emotions and body is hard. You need some tools. Tools are extensions of yourself that allow you to reach some goal, from getting a nail into a block of wood to playing the guitar. If you want to learn to play the guitar, you need the strings, the tuning fork, the instructions, a teacher, and music. You also need discipline, willingness to put in effort, readiness to enjoy the first time you play On Top of Old Smokey, and a belief that someday you might play in a band or do a cool blues riff. You need feedback, support, and an audience. You need to listen to music that has the sound you want to have. All of those are tools, because they help you do the job of building yourself into a guitarist.

Using the toolbox for Sarah's Window isn't all that different. Some discipline to get you to pick up the practice every so often, or to use it when you can, is important. Discipline gets easier the more you get out of it, just as it is easier to practice once the music begins to sound decent. The word practice fits here, too. Keep practicing doing things. The results come from practicing as well as thinking about it. There is also a need for effort against inertia or denial, and some trust that thinking about all this will be worth the work. So those are tools also.

At the same time, another important tool is easing up. You don't keep playing the guitar when your fingers are bleeding. Don't get all in your head about the process, or despair when nothing seems to be happening or getting fixed. The process is easy but the way it works is complicated. Give it time to work. A guitarist isn't made over night, either.

Another tool will be what you have *written down*. Maybe sometimes those who can do so might want to draw what they have understood. Or you can do it as a group or a pair, trading ideas and encouraging each other to keep going. Catherine and I took the Window on as a shared activity, each week discussing what had happened to us in each pane. After a while it became second nature, and then the whole thing would fall by the wayside for a while. But eventually it was firmly enough established as habit that it could be picked up by either of us when we needed it. So, doing it together was a useful tool as well.

You might want to make a list of your own tools, and then in the manner of those Medieval monks, put them in different places in an imaginary toolbox. You will remember what you have, and you can trade one tool out for another when the other isn't the right one. For example, if you get off the track and start to feel anxious about not having cleaned out the house, you might get out the "ease up tool," or maybe the "discipline tool" to focus on another part of the Window. Are you beating yourself up in your same old-fashioned way? Did you talk to someone who has this all wrapped up and you hated them for being so organized? Why did it make you so upset? Where is that on the Window?

Soon, it will be as if you are going to Lowe's or Home Depot every week. New tools will show up in your toolbox. Dreams may prove to be tools sometimes. You might find tools to manage difficult conversations, arguments, confusion, the sudden and unfortunate arrival of something unexpected—something like slowing your breathing or walking away. You might find you like the tool of looking things up on the internet, or consulting with professionals, like home organizers and downsizers to figure out what you can do about parting with things you love. You might like the plain and simple tool of just getting off the dime and doing something.

Sometimes, moments of happiness might knock like a delivery at the back door. These are not much different from the beautiful songs you can finally learn to play on the guitar.

## The Results

If you don't make it a burden, after a while Sarah's Window can just become a way you think about matters, plan, or take care of a time where you feel out of sorts or angry. If you want to take it farther, it will let you. It can become a spiritual practice, or a way to clear out your house without getting too upset. It is for you to decide.

The results of some discipline like Sarah's Window are often strange, subtle, and unanticipated. They aren't even necessarily about the future. Your list of results along the way might include, perhaps surprisingly: greater patience, more energy, comfort with silence, and greater tolerance. You may be less anxious about the future and more willing to see what can be done about it as well as what can't. You might not need to fall for schemes to keep yourself young forever or that offer a permanent cruise lifestyle. You might also stay mentally clear and focused enough about your plans that you will retain the right to run your life for a long time.

You might also find that you are able to manage increasing simplification: simpler living in a smaller place, maybe a general satisfaction with life, even happiness, as you let go of what you can't have and accept the benefits—however small—of what you do have. You don't need to put enlightenment, peace that passes all understanding, spiritual awakening, conversion, or any end-state on a to-do list somewhere. You won't need to focus on any of that. It may not be your thing, or it may. Whatever you believe, the whole life thing might begin to make more sense or feel fine as it is.

Sarah's Window, with its lists, tools, and results, is among other things a way to keep away from or reduce depression, ennui, anxiety, anger, guilt, deep grieving, the weakening of resolve and body, exhaustion, and many other states of mind and muscle that can accompany aging. Rather than focusing on these, you can focus on what is right in front of you today, this hour, now. If you are anxious, simplify or reorganize your living room, or make a plan for where someone else might move the furniture for you in exchange for a blueberry pie or a bag of potato chips. Make a plan for anything at all. Go outside or turn to face the window and focus on the sky. You have to go on, like it or not; so just do that. The future, the ennui, and all of that will still be there, but it will slowly cease to be the main focus of your thoughts or feelings, at least for a while. And you will have gotten something done in the meantime. More bravely, sit and ask your mood what it wants. There is a reason for it, even sometimes for depression.

You may also notice that if you try to keep focused on more than one perspective of the Window, you can lessen the effects of one area of upset with thought about the others. If you are anxious and sad about having to get rid of your favorite sofa, maybe you can think about how to focus on contributing it to someone who needs it. The painful parts can become easier to bear if other actions can balance them out. To focus on the emotional or physical pain too much will make fear appear along with self-pity, and these will not only make you unhappy, but they will exasperate all those around you. And you will not feel in the least at peace.

You can't always let go of the feelings of grief and depression that often accompany aging. "Pulling up your socks" may move from a metaphor to a real struggle. People's admonitions are well-meant, but if they don't fit, don't wear them. If they are actually pointing to a problem you find overwhelming as if you could solve it tomorrow, maybe you can change the task they suggest to one you can do and on which you can make some progress. Or at least, that effort might change the channel for a while. If everything seems to be going wrong at once, maybe you can go deep and see just why it is so painful. Down there, it is likely to just ease up into an old story you have told yourself for years.

If you pay attention to all the positive contributions that aging can allow you to offer others, or how you can still enjoy the company of a friend or a visitor who wakes you out of your doldrums, you might find yourself less concerned with your own problems and more concerned with others. You can fulfill a species imperative to care and connect, which will calm you and send you forward.

All of this is slow work, and it needs constant attention. We need constant attention, and the only one who can really give it to us is ourselves. In the end, we are the architects and engineers of our own lives, all the way through. It's just that the materials keep changing.

So don't give up. This is a way to approach aging in a realistic way that uses what Sarah discovered as a key. It isn't from a lab or a think tank. It is from the experience of a woman who had the mind, the insight, and the generosity to show us what was going to happen and what we needed to do not to be overwhelmed by it. It took Sarah a lifetime really, to weave together all the teachings of her life and death. She would be happy to know that someone might find her story a way to do the same, and with time to live the blossoming results.

# Chapter Ten:
# A Spiritual Way of Aging

*If anything is worth doing, do it with
all your heart.*

### Gautama Buddha

Adding this chapter to the end of the book may be
confusing, so let me try to explain why it is here right at the
beginning of it. The way of working with the Window this
book has described thus far is very practical. Even its deeper
parts have practical goals and practical connections to the
other perspectives. The whole of Sarah's Window is to help
you to prepare for getting old by knowing yourself and what
is coming and putting them together.

There is also another way to work with the Window for
those who have a spiritual bent or perhaps a spiritual
practice. It is not better than the other, and in fact, the other
may be essential to using Sarah's Window in this way.
It is just an example of the many ways the Window can be
adapted to your own predilections and preferences.

If the first use of the Window gives practical answers to
how I am going to manage old age, the second lets me look
into and fold the larger questions of life into what I do.
For those for whom existential and metaphysical questions
grow more important as the end of a lifetime approaches,
this is a way to look into those questions and perhaps live
into the answers.

The spiritual use of the Window combines the practical version of it with a more spiritually focused version. It doesn't change anything about the model or its categories, just focuses them on living a spiritual life as a way of aging.

Using the Window in this way may depend on how much time and freedom from outer responsibilities you can afford. Sometimes it becomes easier the more physically limited you are. It requires some time alone and going deeper than normal, though the "caring and connecting" perspective does not allow the life of a hermit.

Some people feel something in the background of a worldly life and wonder what else there might be. With this approach to the Window, it is possible to develop a spiritual or expanded view of life in a relatively structured way. Will it work for a lifetime? I can't say yet. It is perhaps like taking a new medication that has never been tested on old people.

This third focus may be the most fulfilling and useful use of Sarah's Window to some people, and irrelevant or meaningless to others. It is demanding and requires significant commitment. Its goal is to create a spiritually committed life of discipline that allows for using the last stage of life as an exploration of something larger than oneself.

As Sarah's story revealed, even with nothing more than a calmer mind and less need for control, it is possible to let go of many impossible dreams or demands, and find other, more fundamental ones.

Going beyond that, it may be possible to experience the space that is left when all else is still, truly still, when all the needs are set aside and the anger is as well, when even joy is accepted as fleeting. The last and best encounters of a lifetime might be experiences that are deeper and more real than others you have known. They step beyond all you know into a world you haven't seen or felt before, however you might have suspected or glimpsed its presence. This discovery may offer the first glimmerings of what you might find when you have left it.

Going beyond regular perception and worldly beliefs requires a full commitment to the daily practice of the same four dimensions of Sarah's Window, just more intensely and with a different purpose.

The spiritual form of Sarah's Window is, as it is often called in religious traditions, a *practice.* It requires simplifying to find the time to sit silently, study, act mindfully, and focus on your task. At the same time, it also requires one to contribute compassionately to others, knowing how they suffer. Practice is also about helping as much as it is about understanding. The world is meant to be a source of joy, whoever is in it and however it feels. That joy is to be shared.

This approach is an aspiration and a lodestar, not a guarantee of a sudden splash into happiness or even peace. It is a way of life, and only slowly, intentionally, does it also become a path of fulfillment. The good news is that each step, as Sarah found even on her first few, feels better.

For people of faith, a serious focus on the perspectives

offered in the four window panes may be a way to deepen that faith, as in finding the elusive peace that passes all understanding, letting go and letting God, or having a direct experience of the divine or the world without names that limit our understanding of it. It may feel like a call to explore the meanings, texts and interpretations behind beliefs thousands of years old, seeing what experiences and clarity they give.

Atheists and agnostics can use this approach to fill out their ideas of how to live in the universe fully, God or no God. The universe may be experienced as something different without a god, but it does not disappear. Is there a universe that science can fully explain and show us our place in it? Or will just looking carefully at all we experience illuminate our lives?

All of these approaches could be said to bring a happiness not based on things or ideas of who you are, but what is beyond you and inside you, as described in George Harrison's song, *Within You and Without You*:

> *When you've seen beyond yourself then you may find*
> *Peace of mind is waiting there.*

Overall, Sarah's Window used in this way can help to expand certain ways of thinking and experiencing and consciously decrease others, so that whatever happens can be folded into a whole that feels encompassing and less fraught, and makes many mysteries increasingly intelligible. Some questions may be answered or may become irrelevant, like, "What is the meaning of life?" or, "Why am I here?"

It is interesting to discover that working in this way is similar to what spiritual masters do: they give up a normal life for a life of discipline, insight, compassion, and generosity in order to see what is there beyond the life that they have found insufficient or unfulfilling. As we age, we can indeed build our lives around the same goals; that is the point of Sarah's Window. In that regard, we may have it easy. Much of the simplifying, going deep, giving of ourselves, and even opening our hearts to others that spiritual masters take on can easily become ways of perceiving our own aging, not as matters of sacrifice, but of spiritual growth.

Taking this approach to using Sarah's Window may move a person down the path that monks and mystics aspire to. There is good reason to be happy about that; the expanded views that may come after we die are waiting now, so why not use the head start that aging and the Window can give us to look for them now?

Using the model of Sarah's Window to take a deeper dive into life, you can use the same questions and activities described earlier, just with a tighter focus. Maybe you will want to examine or expand your sense of caring and connecting with others, but if you are having trouble with that, you may be "out of balance" with one or more of the other perspectives.

Again, no one use or understanding of Sarah's Window is better than the other; each fits different temperaments, different circumstances, and different interests. Sarah had little interest in a full dive into the disciplined, committed spiritual life of a monastic; she was happy to see how a spiritual awareness came out of unintended and intentional changes in her life. She had too much to do and too little time to live a life committed to only one thing, and nor did it suit her. It is all a matter of choice.

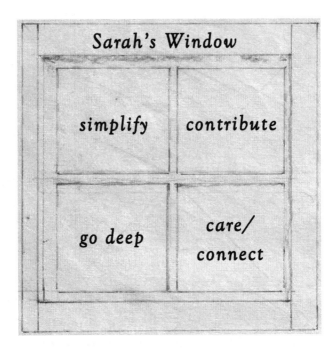

# Afterword

Much more can be said and developed in the use of Sarah's Window, including by you. In addition to Sarah's story, this book offers an introduction to the Window concept only, based upon the experiences of a woman who shaped the framework by allowing us to document the last challenges and discoveries of her life. Both approaches to working with Sarah's Window can be taken further, and then even further, or left where they work best.

In the next months, these more refined uses of the Window will be developed at, *www.responsibleoldageanddeath.com.* The blog includes a special category for *The Last, Best Lessons*. Articles there begin with further development of the practical use of the four panes of Sarah's Window and how to make use of them more fully, with specific questions that fit the exercises described earlier. Discussions about how to use Sarah's Window as a tool of spiritual discipline will come along after. The site allows for discussions and guest contributors. You can subscribe or just check in at *www.responsibleoldageanddeath.com* from time to time.

If you would like to take the exploration of any parts of this book further, please check the *Resources* section that follows. It lists current and classic texts in the fields of aging, dying, aging and wisdom, ways to contribute, the practicalities of old age, and spiritual practices. There is also a list of websites and blogs that will expand your understanding of this approach to the subject.

These resources have been invaluable in the writing of this book; many of the ideas and perspectives presented here have come indirectly, if not directly, from them as well as from notes, conversations and discussions with Sarah and many others who knew, loved, and worked with her.

A last word: Catherine and I began to use Sarah's Window two years ago. It has become a background element of our lives. Writing this book has given us many more ideas about how to use the Window more fully, and how we might be more honest with ourselves. This is to say that we aspire to live this approach, but often are woefully inadequate at it. We are still learning. Don't think we are telling you what to do. We are telling ourselves what to do, and hope it helps you, too, as Sarah wanted.

# Resources for Further Exploration: Suggested Readings

**Louise Aronson**
*Elderhood: Redefining Aging, Transforming Medicine, Reimagining Life*
Bloomsbury Publishing, 2019
A prominent, knowledgeable geriatrician challenges the prevailing view of aging, particularly old-aging, as undesirable. This comprehensive work offers Aronson's insights and knowledge about the medical and social aspects of old age, based on her personal and professional experiences. She views elderhood as a respected and significant life stage, arguing that some of what we dread about it is within our control.

**William Bridges**
*The Way of Transition: Embracing Life's Most Difficult Moments*
Da Capo Press, 2001
One of several of Bridge's books on transitions.
Most dealt with transitions in organizations; this one explores his painful experience with change after his first wife died, when he found himself "stripped down to the studs." He offers up his intensely personal discovery about transition: the neutral zone between endings and beginnings is where the real work is.

**Katy Butler**

*The Art of Dying Well: A Practical Guide to a Good End of Life*
Scribner, 2019
A guide to making the most of your life and living well at the end. Butler describes changes or "situations" to expect as we grow older, and organizes them chronologically in seven chapters, each devoted to a different stage of later life. This approach leads to a fuller understanding of the emotional, physical and spiritual tasks of aging that can lead to a good, or at least better, death.

**Ira Byock, M.D.**

*Dying Well: Peace and Possibilities at the End of Life*
The Berkeley Publishing Group, 1997
*The Best Care Possible: A Physician's Quest to Transform Care Through the End of Life*
The Penguin Group, 2012
Profound insights and experiences of a hospice and palliative care physician in meeting patients' needs at the end of life. Byock makes clear his opposition to the medical-aid-in dying movement, arguing that end-of-life care must change so that physical pain and suffering are managed, and agonizing deaths are alleviated. This book offers insights into his energy and compassion for working with the dying and his perspectives on "death with dignity."

**Martha Calihan, MD**
*A Death Lived*
BookBaby, 2020
A physician's experiences along the journey of her husband's illness and death. Calihan documents her struggle with her role as wife and physician as she provides end-of-life care and prepares herself and her husband for the inevitable end. The story reveals her deep curiosity about what happens when we die, and her life-changing experience at her husband's death.

**Richard Carlson, Ph. D.**
*Don't Sweat the Small Stuff...and it's all Small Stuff:*
*Simple Ways to Keep the Little Things from Taking Over Your Life*
Hyperion, 1997
One hundred suggestions from a psychotherapist-author on keeping yourself from being overcome by life and waking up to what is before you. This work lives on as a notable accomplishment for a man who died at age 45.

**Rabbi Rachel Cowan & Dr. Linda Thal**
*Wise Aging: Living with Joy, Resilience & Spirit*
Behrman House, Inc. 2015
An engaging and thoughtfully organized book, each chapter containing essays, poems, insights, journaling exercises, and reflective questions that can be used as a workbook for individuals or groups. Discussions and exercises largely reflect Jewish principles and teachings, drawing also from other spiritual practices.

**Harold Coward, Editor**
*Life After Death in World Religions*
Orvis Books   1997
Observations on life-after-death practices and beliefs among various major Eastern, Western, ancient and contemporary religions. This introductory collection is drawn from lectures from a community of internationally recognized religious scholars.

**Barbara Ehrenreich**
*Natural Causes: An Epidemic of Wellness, The Certainty of Dying, and Killing Ourselves to Live Longer*
Hachette Book Group, Inc.  2018
A provocative look at questionable practices in the medical profession that keep people, particularly the aging, alive and not well; our fixation on fitness and wellness programs that yield questionable results; and the current misplaced over-emphasis on "active" or "productive" aging.
The author's underlying message: death is inescapable and far less scary than our obsession with avoiding it.

**Margaret Morganroth Gullette**
*Ending Ageism or How Not to Shoot Old People*
Rutgers University Press, 2017
A frank and compelling consideration of the inequities old people face in our current culture: either ignoring or extolling their wisdom robs them of their humanity. This is an atypical treatise on the challenges of aging, and a call to confront harmful and demeaning attitudes, often unspoken, toward older people. The author portends that overcoming agism will be a key imperative for our time.

**Joel Havemann**

*A Life Shaken: My Encounter with Parkinson's Disease*
The Johns Hopkins University Press, 2002
A first-person account of journalist Joel Havemann's life and determination to live with Parkinson's—from 1990 until his death in 2020 at age 76. Written 12 years into his disease, this book covers not just Havemann's early years with the disease, but the its long-term "trajectory," and his difficult and dignified struggle along the way.


**Harold S. Kushner**

*Living a Life That Matters: Resolving the Conflict*
*Between Conscience and Sucess*
Alfred A. Knopf, 2001
A book by a congregational rabbi and author about our need to know, as we age and face death, that our lives have meaning and that we have made a difference. He emphasizes that we can counter this  perception by reviewing the values we upheld in life and the love we leave behind.


**Stephen Levine**

*A Year to Live: How to Live This Year as If It Were Your Last*
Bell Tower, 1997
A book on the power of daily mindful living. For one year, the author lived his life as though preparing for his death, documenting each month of his journey, anticipating it as an invaluable experience. Levine invites the reader to join in and provides a year's worth of strategies and meditations to prepare for living one year as if it were their last.

**Margareta Magnusson**
*The Gentle Art of Swedish Death Cleaning: How to Free Yourself
and Your Family from a Lifetime of Clutter*
Scribner, 2018
A short book with a thoughtful concept: clean up after
yourself before you die. It is a reminder that cleaning up and
minimalizing our stuff is not only a kindness, but a
responsibility to those we leave behind. Here is practical
advice and philosophical musings on a process more freeing
than overwhelming.

**BJ Miller, M.D., and Shoshana Berger**
*A Beginner's Guide to the End: Practical Advice for Living Life
and Facing Death*
Simon & Schuster, 2019
Written by a physician who faced death in his youth, and
whose changed relationship with death led him to become a
hospice and palliative care physician. The book provides a
comprehensive yet practical list of to-do's for dealing with illness; coming to grips with all aspects of your own
(or another's) dying: planning for it, and learning how to
prepare for death when it is close, and then complete. This
valuable guide provides answers to most, if not all, questions
about preparing for our final journey.

**Diane Rehm**

*When My Time Comes: Conversations About Whether Those Who Are Dying Should Have the Right to Determine When Life Should End*

2020 Alfred A. Knopf

Twenty insightful interviews with those connected directly and indirectly with issues of medical aid in dying.

This companion book to the 2021 PBS documentary "When My Time Comes" presents a balanced mix of people and perspectives and encourages clear-headed debate on the topic of end-of life and aid-in-dying measures. The book is a valuable contribution to the death-with-dignity movement from one who witnessed the lingering death of her husband in 2014.

**Lewis Richmond**

*Aging as a Spiritual Practice : A Contemplative Guide to Growing Older and Wiser*

Gotham Books, 2012

A guide to aging well from a Zen Buddhist priest and meditation teacher that can be used in individual or group practice. Each chapter offers Buddhist-influenced spiritual practices and lessons and contemplative reflections that allow deeper exploration of ideas about wise aging.

**Zalman Schachter-Shalomi and Ronald S. Miller**
*From Age-ing to Sage-ing: A Revolutionary Approach to Growing Older*
Grand Central Publishing-Hatchett Book Group, 1995
A classic work of the wise-aging movement that focuses on changing the aging paradigm and creating new ways to stay socially useful. The author advocates for pursuing a fulfilling, creative, and meaningful life in old age, and using our unique experiences to take on a more sage-like presence as we connect with younger generations.

**John M. Vine**
*A Parkinson's Primer: An Indispensable Guide to Parkinson's Disease for Patients and Their Families*
Paul Dry Books, 2017
A book about Parkinson's Disease from someone who received the diagnosis in 2004 at age 60. It covers all aspects of the disease; symptoms and therapies and helpful resources; myths about PD; and a "Why Me?" chapter.
He includes interviews with patients and loved ones, whose sto¬ries and advice he shares in hopes of helping others.

# Organizations, Blogs, and Podcasts

**Compassion & Choices**
*www.compassionandchoices.org*
An organization—"the nation's older, largest and most active non-profit"—that "improves care, expands options, and empowers everyone to chart their end-of-life journey and ensure that their decisions are honored."

**Death with Dignity**
*www.deathwithdignity.org*
**Death with Dignity National Center**
An organization whose mission is "to promote death with dignity laws based on our model legislation, the Oregon Death with Dignity Act, both to both to provide an option for dying individuals and to stimulate nationwide improvements in end-of-life care."

**Final Exit Network**
*www.finalexitnetwork.com*
An organization that supports right to a death with dignity. Services are free, and include "educating qualified individuals in practical, peaceful ways to end their lives" and offering consultation on ways to make sure advanced directives are honored. They also have developed an advance directive to use to prevent the dying from being hand fed against their wishes, including those with dementia.

**Sage-ing International**
*www.sage-ing.org*
Email: information@sage-ing.org
A community of elders exploring new ways of aging, which they call "conscious aging." Once a networking vehicle for professionals, this non-profit organization offers learning and service programs for older adults that encourage using later years as a time for "sage-ing" and becoming active and productive members of society.

**The Conversation Project**
*www.theconversationproject.org*
A "public engagement initiative with a goal...to help everyone talk about their wishes for care through the end of life, so those wishes can be understood and respected." It emphasizes the need for people to share how they want to live "through the end of our lives..." and to have over-the-kitchen table discussions with those closest to us— before it is too late.

**Sages & Seekers**
*www.sagesandseekers.org*
A national program offering intergenerational programs as a forum for young adults (seekers) and elders (sages) to develop empathy and deeper understanding for each other through conversation. Sages & Seekers programs "strive to combat social isolation and dissolve age-related segregation within our communities, while meeting the universal and compelling need of both young adults and elders to make sense of their lives..."

# Blogs and Podcasts

*www.anthrochap.com*
A blog for being responsible about getting older, planning for the coming difficult periods of life, and looking for grace and the sacred in the time that is left.

*www.changingaging.org*
A "multi-blog publishing platform" offering perspectives that challenge conventional views of aging and promotes the idea that aging is a key part of development and growth.
They encourage submissions from the community at large.

*www.deathanddyingchronicles.com*
A hospice nurse's blog created to answer the many questions patients and families have when they have been told they do not have long to live.

*www.legacycafe.podbean.com*
A podcast hosted by writer Robb Lucy that encourages people to create and share their written legacies they will leave for their descendants, loved ones, and future generations. The site offers a variety of podcasts by experts in the field of legacy writing, including authors, motivational speakers, and gerontologists.

*www.lewisrichmond.com/aging-blog/*
A blog that provides a forum for readers of the book
"Aging as a Spiritual Practice," as well as the interested
public, to read about Lewis Richmond's latest thoughts on
aging as a transformational process and to learn about the
latest aging research.

*www.sage-ing.org/blog*
Blogs at this site are written by Sage-ing international
members. Topics include life after death and the effects of
the recent pandemic on the path of growth for conscious
elders. Guidelines for submissions are included.

*www.memorywell.com*
A digital platform designed for healthcare providers, this site
offer the services of professional writers who interview
patients to produce brief and insightful stories that allow
providers and others to better understand patients and
residents. Although a for-profit endeavor, the site offers
helpful information and testimonials about a tool that
connects us to people's basic humanity.

Made in the USA
Middletown, DE
07 October 2021

49841352R00128